My Hope In Hell

by
Jens Reuter

Copyright © 2014 by Jens Reuter

All rights reserved. This book or any portion thereof may not be reproduced or used in any manner whatsoever without the express written permission of the publisher except for the use of brief quotations in a book review or scholarly journal.

Publisher: Jens Reuter
hellbook@gmail.com
11623 46 Ave
Edmonton,
T6H0A6
Distributer: Lulu.com

ISBN 978-1-312-83957-1

For Kathryn

Introduction

It was in India that I began to think about hell. It wasn't the passionate sermons of the pastor we stayed with that did it. It was the people. Millions and millions of them crowded the streets, most of them poorer than we can even imagine. And as I saw them live and suffer and march inevitably towards death, I realized that if what I believe is true, then all of them will someday burn in hell. The vast majority of Indians are Hindus. They will never accept Jesus as their personal Savior. Most of them will never be told to accept Jesus as Savior. They will simply, if my theology is correct, eke out a living, pay homage to false gods, die hoping be reincarnated into a better life, and find themselves locked in the bowels of hell for eternity. Millions of people, doomed from birth.

I went to see the Taj Mahal, and like many visitors I was stunned by its beauty and intrigued by its story. The Taj Mahal was built for love, dedicated by a Muslim King to his favorite wife, to ensure her memory lived on forever. I remembered that she herself would live forever too, presumably in hell. I wondered what she thought of the monument, if it dulled her agony to know that people came to see her tomb. I wondered if she derived comfort from her husband's presence in hell, or if damnation had turned them both into horrible monsters in which the love had long since died. I wondered if she had such thoughts at all, or if the burning agony of hellfire consumed her mind as well as her body. And although I knew nothing about the woman at all, I decided then and there that her fate was unfair and that God should not be burning her forever.

We Christians have a terrible belief which is called "hell", an idea so bizarre that popular culture has minded endless humor from it. We read it in our Bibles and preach it from our pulpits. Most of mankind- so many churches tell us- is doomed forever to an awful place that we call "hell." Even worse, perhaps, is that the one who puts them there is the one we worship and adore and point to as the wellspring of everything good: God Himself. Thinking too much about hell turns the love that I should have for God into anger, disgust, and just a sliver of fear, in case God should choose such a fate for me. My oldest friend, who writes a blog under the pen name "Jacob", has this to say: *"I marvel that Christians are able to cope with this belief... just to function in this world with the knowledge that some people you love will suffer for eternity is a herculean task. I don't know how people can sleep or laugh or work or worship God while believing in hell."* Yet hell is a key doctrine of Christianity, and indeed, of many religions. I speak as a Christian, but most faiths have some conception of hell.

 A lot of Christians choose, quite simply, to ignore their beliefs of hell. We talk about "the lost" or the "unsaved" without allowing ourselves to think about what that really means. I remember a conversation I had once with a Christian friend, over the death of a non-Christian acquaintance. "We don't say much about it, do we?" he asked. "We can't say that he's in a better place, because we don't believe that. Why don't we ever say the opposite: that he's burning in hell? That's what we believe... isn't it?"

 I imagine many people have had such conversations, punctuated with awkward silences. I imagine many people have had to deal with these questions. Never mind that the theology of hell is a critical part of our belief system, a theological position we may be able to defend chapter-and-verse with our Bibles in hand. The personal questions are harder to deal with. How can we look into the eyes of a child and tell them their unsaved mother is burning in hell? And so we don't answer. Not really, anyway. We avert our eyes, shuffle our feet, and mutter something about "God knows best" and "it's all up to Him." We deal with the horrors of hell by ignoring them, by sweeping them under the rug, by pretending they don't exist; the theological equivalent of hoping that if we don't go to the doctor, that lump in our flesh won't turn out to be cancer.

I, for one, am not satisfied with this approach to hell. My faith itself threatens to erode if I cannot reconcile my understanding of a loving God with my understanding of hell. I wish to examine the doctrine, to study it, to think about it. To consider both what the Bible says about hell, and what the church (both today and throughout history) has believed. I want to examine the effect the doctrine of hell has on our lives, both positively and negatively. I don't want to blindly accept what is taught from the pulpit, but neither can I lightly dismiss what other wiser and better Christians believe.

I am not the only one who is "rethinking" hell. In fact, much of the church is doing so, and many Christian leaders of modern times have nontraditional views of hell. Among the people I know, I conducted an informal survey, asking people to explain hell for me. My acquaintances are hardly a representative sample of the Christian world but they do include Canadians, Americans and South Africans, professionals, university students and homemakers, upper-class persons and former street gangsters, liberal Christians and conservative ones. I was surprised by the wide and often diverse understandings of hell these people had. (I should also mention that many of my Christian friends claimed only a very limited understanding of hell, or said they hadn't thought about it much. One remarked that my question had made her realize that she didn't believe in hell.)

Some of the more interesting thoughts, necessarily paraphrased to the best of my recollection are as follows:

"Where is it burning, dark, and with no way out? The center of the Earth. That's where hell is."

"Imagine two banquet halls, where people have only really long forks to feed themselves. In one hall everyone is happy, because they are feeding each other. That is heaven. In the other room, everyone is starving, bleeding and cut up, because they are only trying to feed themselves with those long forks. That is hell."

"Hell is wanting to tear out each of your hairs individually for eternity because you are so frustrated that you

did not accept salvation when you had the chance."

"There is a type of fire that is invisible, so it burns but does not light up the dark. That's what hell is like. Fire and darkness. That's hell."

"If God sends good people to hell because they don't believe in him, then I wouldn't want to spend eternity with him anyway. That would be hell."

"God doesn't torture people in hell! When Jesus returns, and you realize you don't like what he has to say, that's hell."

"People who are living without God are already in hell. When they die, they just continue the way things are, but it's worse because the blessings of God they enjoy on Earth, even though they don't follow him, will be withdrawn."

"In the end, Jesus will only ask you one question. Do you want to go into heaven? And some people will still say no."

"Once you are born, you are going to hell. That's just where people go, it's part of being human. Christians have a way out."

"Hell is really boring. There won't be any soccer balls to kick around or anything; there is nothing at all to do."

In the end, the existence (or nonexistence) and characteristics of hell are what they are, regardless of what I may think or say or write. God's plans will come to fruition, regardless of my opinions on the matter, and the salvation or damnation of the world does not hinge in any way on my opinion. Nor can I pretend to know better than God what has to be done, to correct the divine plan or offer alternatives to infinite wisdom. All I can strive to do, though I fear my efforts in this case may be hopeless, is to understand.

Why does Hell exist?

Chapter 1

Author: Unknown (chain email).
Setting: A modern university; the final question on a chemistry exam.
Scientific Explanation of Hell
Bonus Question: Is Hell exothermic (gives off heat) or endothermic (absorbs heat)?

Most of the students wrote proofs of their beliefs using Boyle's Law (gas cools when it expands and heats when it is compressed) or some variant.
One student, however, wrote the following:
First, we need to know how the mass of Hell is changing in time. So we
need to know the rate at which souls are moving into Hell and the rate at
which they are leaving. I think that we can safely assume that once a soul gets to Hell, it
will never leave. Therefore, no souls are leaving..
As for how many souls are entering Hell, let's look at the different religions that exist in the world today. Most of these religions state that if you are not a member of their religion, you will go to Hell. Since there is more than one of these religions and since people do not belong to more than one religion, we can project that all souls go to Hell.
With birth and death rates as they are, we can expect the number of souls in hell to increase exponentially. Now, we look at the rate of change of the volume in Hell because Boyle's Law states that in order for the temperature and pressure in Hell to stay the same, the volume of Hell has to expand proportionately as souls

are added

This gives two possibilities:

1. If Hell is expanding at a slower rate than the rate at which souls enter Hell, then the temperature and pressure in Hell will increase until all Hell breaks loose.

2. If Hell is expanding at a rate faster than the rate at which souls enter Hell, then the temperature and pressure will drop until Hell freezes over. So which is it?

If we accept the postulate given to me by Teresa, (Cheerleader Captain and Class valedictorian) during my Freshman year, that, "it will be a cold day in Hell before I go out with you", and take into account the fact that I went out with her last night, then number 2 must be true, and thus I am sure that Hell is exothermic and has already frozen over.

The corollary of this theory is that since Hell has frozen over, it follows that it is not accepting any more souls and is therefore, extinct...leaving only Heaven.

Why does Hell exist

Let us define **Hell**, as briefly and broadly as possible: "After death, some people will suffer for their earthly sins". This statement will encompass, I think, most theological positions on hell.

C.S. Lewis gave three reasons why he felt it necessary to believe in hell: the doctrine of hell "has the full support of Scripture, especially of our Lord's own words; and has always been held by Christendom. And it has the support of Reason." The first two reasons certainly have merit. In the Bible, Jesus talks a lot about hell (though there is controversy what exactly he meant). Secondly, almost all streams of Christianity have some doctrine of future punishment. Even liberal churches generally believe in some sort of hell. Lewis' third suggestion, that hell is reasonable, is a much more controversial proposition.

The necessity of hell's existence is generally explained in one of two ways: as just punishment for sin (thus balancing the scales of justice in the universe), and as man's final rejection of God, and therefore all that is good. These are not mutually exclusive reasons. Rather, since rejection of God is the ultimate sin, they are inextricably entwined.

G.K. Chesterton called the sinfulness of man the one empirically verifiable Christian doctrine, and thousands of years of human history have borne him out. Human beings are selfish, petty, cruel, complacent and violent. Gossip, laziness, drunkenness, lust- our Bible may tell us that these are wrong, but so often they appear as harmless and even fun. The sinfulness of our modern lifestyle is easy to ignore. Renowned Christian writer Philip Yancey suggests that "*the seven deadly sins have become in today's modern world, seven deadly virtues. Our entire greedy grasping world is built on them.*" Sometimes I find it necessary to gain perspective, to see for myself the brutal ends to which such seemingly insignificant sins leads.

My sister works as a physician in South Africa. Every day, she sees those who have succumbed to the sins of promiscuity and are now slowly dying of AIDS. Every day, she sees people covered with terrible wounds, shot and stabbed, beaten because they live in the culture of violence that comes from racism and hatred. For several months I worked in a run-down school in the South African slums, where the teacher felt so hopeless and the students so angry that classrooms were destroyed and left to decay on a regular basis. Drug addicts, searching to finance their terrible habit, scaled the razor-wired fences at night to steal wiring, doorknobs and bathroom taps to sell. The school sits near the boundary between two gang turfs. Every child had stories of ducking gunfire, and every one of the volunteer workers, including myself, was at some point a victim of armed robbery. When I forget the awfulness of sin, I think back to the South African slums. South African Christians have much less trouble understanding hell than Canadians; many of them see hell every day.

I myself work with youths with behavioral problems. For many of them, the foster homes and accompanying schools they live in are the last alternative to prison. I think of the students I worked with, the situations that have placed them where they are. Many of these children have been robbed of their mental abilities by their parent's drinking and by their own drug habits. Many youths are so angry and aggressive they must be physically restrained for the safety of their classmates and teachers. Young women are so depressed we must wrestle paper clips from their fingers to keep them from hurting themselves. I remember a boy so broken down from life, that he smashed his head against a wall, over and over again, desperately seeking release from a world of pain. I remember many, many children saying "I hate myself. I want to die." One even told me "I'm going to die and go to hell, because I am bad." Human sin, both their own and that of their parents, has destroyed the lives of these children. What I see on a small scale, is written large in the pages of history. Two World Wars, the Holocaust, Hitler and Stalin and Mao Zedong, too many genocides to remember and an arms race that could well have destroyed the world. Those of Jesus' day would be horrified to hear what the twentieth century has experienced. On a more everyday basis, my own society eats itself quite literally to death while the third world starves. Human behaviour- human sin- is a horrible stain on the fabric of existence. It is a stain that spreads from every human heart that manifests itself in little everyday cruelties, in laziness and rudeness and commonplace greed, until it explodes on a global scale, causing the world to wonder how we ever got this bad. To say that mankind deserves no punishment at all is to forget the true nature of man. *"We are not righteous; no, not one,* [1] laments the apostle Paul, and it is completely right. Popular theologian R.C. Sproul reminds us that *" If God is holy at all, if God has an ounce of justice in His character, indeed if God exists as God, how could He possibly be anything else but angry with us? We violate His holiness; we insult His justice; we make light of His grace. These things can hardly be pleasing to Him."*

    My conception of justice includes rewards for good behaviours and punishments for bad ones. The very fabric of society incorporates this principle from a very young age, when parents penalize and reward their children to gain appropriate responses. All legal systems are based on this principle. Punishment serves not only as deterrent, but as a morally "right" consequence to evil behaviour. Criminals are taken to prison not only to protect society from them, but because society intuitively feels that their suffering is somehow morally "good". The same phenomenon is visible in the media, from silly action movies where the bad guy "gets it" at the end, to news coverage of sensational crimes, where the public demands that we throw the book at real-life bad guys and make them suffer. Punishment is not a pleasant concept, but most would agree it is a necessary one.

    The punishment of evil is also a religious concept in many faiths. Hinduism and Buddhism have consequences deeply enshrined in the law of karma. What you do must be repaid, if not in this life then by your suffering in the next one. The monotheistic religions generally rely on the Justice of God to make it all work out. *"Vengeance is mine, I will repay"*[2] says the God of the Bible, asking mankind to leave punishment to the One who alone can balance justice and mercy.

    In the Old Testament, God shows great interest in balancing the scales of justice when He deals with the nation of Israel. The Old Testament God is, to quote Yancey again, the Ultimate Behaviourist. The terms are laid out in black and white; obey God and receive rich blessings, long life, victory and comfort. Disobey and reap the whirlwind of famine, destruction and death. Much of the Old Testament tells the stories of those who obeyed and those who did not, with appropriate consequences. The prophets devote significant time to promising vengeance to those who are evil, while God will reward those who have suffered unfairly.

    The Jewish doctrine of hell appeared during Israel's Babylonian captivity, and grew in popularity during the Roman occupation of Israel at the time of Christ. God, it seemed to the Jews, had stopped balancing the scales of Justice. Good Jews suffered and died, and no restitution came. Pastor and writer Rob Bell tells us that the Jewish concept of the afterlife was largely an attempt to solve this fundamental problem; a hope that good would be rewarded and evil punished, in a way that was emphatically not occurring in the physical realm. Belief in the afterlife was still a controversial subject among the Jews when Jesus began his teaching. The Bible records His becoming involved in disputes between those that believed in the afterlife and those that did not. For Jesus however, and those who followed Him, the afterlife was a certainty.

    The Resurrection of the saved, and their eternal life with God, is one of the cornerstone beliefs of Christianity. The final pleasure of heaven is a hope to all who suffer in this life. The final end of the evil, those enemies of God who are not saved, is historically less certain. Contrary to what many conservative Christians believe, the more "liberal" views on hell are as old the Bible itself. In early Christianity, all the common ideas debated today are expressed: that the evil dead disappear from existence, that they are painfully purified in hope that they might someday enter heaven, and that they enter an endless conscious punishment.

    Christianity boldly proclaims that God is willing to forgive, for those who have faith and ask for forgiveness. However, it also proclaims that those who, for whatever reason, are outside of God's forgiveness will face perfect justice. To believe in hell is to believe evil is punished, and that in a world that rewards the strong and the amoral, justice- true justice, as determined by God Himself- is finally served.

    Erwin Lutzer writes: "We all agree that heaven is a comforting doctrine. What is often overlooked is that hell is comforting, too. Newspapers are filled with stories of rape, child abuse, and myriad injustices. Every court case ever tried will be reopened; every action and motive will be meticulously inspected and just retribution meted out. In the presence of an all-knowing God there will be no unsolved murders, no unknown child abductor, and no hidden bribe."

I strongly emphasize Lutzer's words. While we might disagree on what punitive measures are appropriate, we both feel the need for God's justice in an often awful world.

    Eastern (Orthodox) Christianity focuses less on the punitive aspect of hell- as retribution sent by an angry God- than on the inevitable consequence of man's stubborn desire to reject God's grace. Rejection of God is the greatest of all sins, the one sin that succeeds in cutting us off from the Love of God. God is willing, eager, hoping to forgive, but He will not, or cannot, forgive those who refuse the gift of Grace. *"A gift must be accepted"* Philip Yancey explains. When we ask Jesus to leave us, He does, and *"God withdraws, honouring our fatal freedom to ignore Him."* Jesus himself expressed a similar sentiment in the book of John: *"Light came into the world, but men loved darkness more than the light, because their deeds were evil."*[3]

The way Rob Bell explains it "*if at any point God overrides, co-opts, or hijacks the human heart, robbing us of our freedom to choose, then God has violated the very essence of what love even means.*"

It seems that if we choose against God, hell is the "other", the anti-God. C.S. Lewis, who understood hell in such terms, puts it this way: "*There are two kinds of people in the world: those that say to God 'thy will be done', and those to whom God says, in the end, "thy will be done". All that are in hell choose it. Without that self-choice there would be no hell. No soul that seriously and consistently desires joy will ever miss it. Those who seek, find. To those who knock it is opened.*" In his book, The Problem of Pain, he famously argued that "*the doors of hell are locked from the inside*" and that people are in hell because they have made themselves unsuitable for anything else. While nobody relishes being thrown into the lake of fire, not everyone wants to be in the presence of God either. Lewis again: "*In the long run the answer to all those who object to the doctrine of Hell is itself a question: 'What are you asking God to do?' To wipe out their past sins and, at all costs, to give them a fresh start, smoothing every difficulty and offering every miraculous help? But He has done so, on Calvary. To forgive them? They will not be forgiven. To leave them alone? Alas, I am afraid that is what He does.*"

Scripture, in several shocking passages, highlights the actions of people who come into the glorious presence of God, and still choose darkness over the light. Jesus' strongest warnings come in the face of such wilful rejection. Jesus befriended thieves and adulterers, traitors and terrorists, but for one group of sinners he showed his contempt; those who, having seen full proof of his Deity through miraculous means, still choose to reject His teaching. "*Woe to you, Chorazin! Woe to you, Bethsaida!*" Jesus thunders, his eyes flashing, perhaps, more in frustration than rage. "*For if the mighty works which were done in you had been done in Tyre and Sidon, they would have repented long ago in sackcloth and ashes, But I say to you, it will be more tolerable for Tyre and Sidon in the day of Judgement than for you!*" [4]

The greatest offenders are the infamous Pharisees.

Blessed with a lifetime to study the Scriptures, witnesses to signs and wonders that no man could deny, they not only refused to worship Christ; they conspired to kill him. Never before has Jesus been so livid. *"Serpents, brood of vipers! How can you escape the condemnation of hell? Therefore, indeed, I send you prophets, wise men and scribes; some of them you will kill and crucify, and some of them you will scourge in your synagogues and persecute from city to city, that on you may come all the righteous bloodshed on the Earth!"* Soon anger gives way to sadness. *"Oh Jerusalem, Jerusalem, the one who kills the prophets and stones those who are sent to her! How often I wanted to gather your children together, as a hen gathers her chicks under her wings, but you were not willing!"* [5] When you look into the face of love and mercy and turn away, nothing is left but sorrow, pain and destruction.

The most mind-boggling example of all is found in the Book of Revelation, as described in a few terse verses. Regardless of one's framework for understanding this book, the message in this story is chilling. The scene: the end of the Millennium, a thousand-year period in which Satan has been chained, and Christ himself rules over the Earth. It is a time of peace, prosperity and love. It is a time when God can be seen, felt, approached, and understood. (It is, presumably, a time when the book of Revelation can be accurately interpreted, and sermons preached galore on what is about to unfold.) This is, for all intents and purposes, heaven on Earth. Into the blissful scene comes the devil, newly released from his bondage. After a thousand years in chains, giving him ample time to consider the power of God and the consequences of doing evil, Satan is not remorseful. He quickly gathers an army, and the human volunteers are many.

"Now when the thousand years have expired, Satan will be released from his prison and he will go out to deceive the nations which are in the four corners of the earth, Gog and Magog, to gather them together to battle, whose number is as the sand of the sea. They went up on the breadth of the earth and surrounded the camp of the saints and the beloved city. And fire came down from God out of heaven and devoured them." [6]

Even in sight of heaven, it seems, some people want hell.

No passage I know describes the need for hell more than this short story. In the end the enemies of God are given their wish. The next chapter in Revelation discusses the final judgement and the Lake of Fire.

Hell in the Bible

Chapter 2

Author: The Apostle Matthew (chapter 25)
Setting: Jesus preaching to his disciples
"When the Son of Man comes in his glory, and all the angels with him, he will sit on his throne in heavenly glory. All the nations will be gathered before him, and he will separate the people one from another as a shepherd separates the sheep from the goats. He will put the sheep on his right and the goats on his left.

"Then the King will say to those on his right, 'Come, you who are blessed by my Father; take your inheritance, the kingdom prepared for you since the creation of the world. For I was hungry and you gave me something to eat, I was thirsty and you gave me something to drink, I was a stranger and you invited me in, I needed clothes and you clothed me, I was sick and you looked after me, I was in prison and you came to visit me.'

"Then the righteous will answer him, 'Lord, when did we see you hungry and feed you, or thirsty and give you something to drink? When did we see you a stranger and invite you in, or naked and clothe you? When did we see you sick or in prison and go to visit you?' "The King will reply, 'I tell you the truth, whatever you did for one of the least of these brothers of mine, you did for me.'

"Then he will say to those on his left, 'Depart from me, you who are cursed, into the eternal fire prepared for the devil and his angels. For I was hungry and you gave me nothing to eat, I was thirsty and you gave me nothing to drink, I was a stranger and you did not invite me in, I needed clothes and you did not clothe me, I was sick and in prison and you did not look after me.'

"They also will answer, 'Lord, when did we see you hungry or thirsty or a stranger or needing clothes or sick or in prison, and

did not help you?' "He will reply, 'I tell you the truth, whatever you did not do for one of the least of these, you did not do for me.'
"Then they will go away to eternal punishment, but the righteous to eternal life."[7]

What does the Bible say about Hell?

Many Christians, who feel intense discomfort with the doctrine of eternal hell, continue to affirm it because hell is a topic of Scripture. Francis Chan, who states that he is sickened by hell and wants to erase it from the Bible, nevertheless concludes that *"It's incredibly arrogant to pick and choose which incomprehensible truths we embrace. No one wants to ditch God's plan of redemption, even though it doesn't make sense to us. Neither should we erase God's revealed plan of punishment because it doesn't sit well with us. As soon as we do this, we are putting God's actions in submission to our own reasoning, which is a ridiculous thing for the clay to do."* Perhaps, the most important question to ask, then, is what the Scriptures actually say.

References to hell are surprisingly sparse in Scripture, especially given the importance of hell in Christian theology. The Old Testament, the larger portion of the Bible, does not speak about hell at all. In fact, in one of the great ironies of religious history, Judaism was one of very few religions who had no real theology of the afterlife until about 400 BC.

Readers of the King James Bible might be surprised to learn this. Older versions of the King James featured the world "hell" in many Old Testament books, but they have now been more accurately translated. Rather than heaven or hell, Old Testament Jews believed in Sheol, the world of the dead, likely a place with no conscious sensation at all. Once erroneously translated "hell" in many Bibles, Sheol is better rendered "grave", as in the NIV and most other modern translations. Rather than the world of the damned, Sheol is a place for the righteous and wicked alike, the final resting place of all humanity. The book of Ecclesiastes gives a good portrayal of this early Jewish understanding of death:

All share a common destiny - the righteous and the

wicked, the good and the bad, the clean and the unclean, those who offer sacrifices and those who do not. As it is with the good man, so with the sinner; as it is with those who take oaths, so with those who are afraid to take them. This is the evil in everything that happens under the sun: The same destiny overtakes all. The hearts of men, moreover, are full of evil and there is madness in their hearts while they live, and afterward they join the dead. Anyone who is among the living has hope - even a live dog is better off than a dead lion! For the living know that they will die, but the dead know nothing; they have no further reward, and even the memory of them is forgotten. Their love, their hate and their jealousy have long since vanished.[8]

Rather than "discovering" hell in inspired Scripture, Judaism seems to have learned the concept from other religious systems during the Jewish exile in Babylonian. Popular Christian author Brian McLaren lists Mesopotamian, Egyptian, Zoroastrian and Greek religious beliefs in the afterlife as influencing the Jewish tradition. Belief in post-mortem consequences in Scripture first appears briefly in the book of Daniel, written about 400 years before Christ: "*Many of those who sleep in the dust of the ground will awake, these to everlasting life, but the others to disgrace and everlasting contempt.*"[9]

At the time of Jesus' life, religious leaders in Israel were divided over their belief or disbelief in an afterlife of any sort. Brian McLaren explains: *The Sadducees were the more conservative Jews who resisted this mixing [of religious belief]. They wouldn't accept Persian ideas such as hell, heaven, and angels. For them a person dies and that's it, with no resurrection. The more liberal or progressive Jews were known as the Pharisees... the Pharisees integrated these Persian-Zoroastrian concepts into their belief system.*

Bible teaching about hell is to be found only in the writings of a few New Testament authors. The books of Matthew and Revelation are the prime locations where the word "hell" and the "lake of fire" can be found. Mark and Luke have a few references to hell; they also tell several parables that Matthew has, but without the hellish finish. Luke also records the famous parable of Lazarus and Dives. The book of Revelation aside, the apostles Paul and John never use the word hell in any of its forms. Paul makes one mention to "eternal separation" from God. The book of James has one usage (describing an evil tongue as "set on fire by hell"). The book of 1 Peter uses the word Tartarus (often translated "hell") from Greek mythology to describe the punishment of angels. Both Peter and Jude make references to God's judgement often interpreted as taking place after death.

To increase the confusion, no single Greek word for "hell" is used in scripture. In addition to "Tartarus" (which occurs once), the words translated as "hell" in the New King James are "Hades" and "Gehenna". "Hades" is likewise from the Greek religious system and refers to the world of the dead. Hades is sometimes equivalent to the Hebrew "Sheol" (the world of the dead) but at other times (notably the Parable of Lazarus and the Rich Man) it is portrayed as a place of conscious suffering for the wicked. When Jesus prophesies that *"the gates of hell will not prevail against the church"*[10] he is using the word Hades. In the book of Revelation, Hades is emptied, its occupants are summoned before God, and Hades itself is thrown into the lake of fire and destroyed, a veritable burning of hell by hell. Many conservative Christians (Jack van Impe, Erwin Lutzer and J.P. Moreland among them) understand Hades as a sort of holding cell, from which the wicked dead will eventually be removed for final sentencing into a more permanent hell after the final judgement at the end of time.

The other Biblical word for hell is "Gehenna." (Hades and Gehenna are mentioned 11 and 12 times respectively by Jesus, according to Jack van Impe)
Gehenna (genhinnom) began as the name of a literal place, the valley of Ben- Hinnom outside the city of Jerusalem. Scottish theologian William Barclay describes the sordid history of this place as follows: *The Valley of Hinnom... was notorious as the place where Ahaz had introduced into Israel the fire-worship of the pagan god Molech, to whom little children were burned in the fire. 'He made offerings in the valley of the son of Hinnom, and made his sons pass through fire' (2 Chronicles 28:3). Josiah, the reforming king, had stamped out that worship, and had ordered that the valley should be forever an accursed place. 'He defiled Topeth, which is in the valley of Ben-Hinnom, so that no one*

would make a son or daughter pass through fire as an offering to Molech'.[11]

In the eyes of the Israelites the place was defiled, much like an Auschwitz or a Dachau is today. It became Jerusalem's garbage dump. Gehenna became the perfect metaphor for a place of sin and punishment. Many of the Biblical descriptions of hell are quite literally fulfilled in the Valley of Ben- Hinnom. The garbage was perpetually being burned, and among the leaping flames, worms and maggots fed on the garbage. Gehenna truly was the place where *"the worm does not die, and the fire is not quenched"*[12]. The bodies of criminals, unworthy of a decent burial, were thrown into the pile to be decayed or consumed. Dark smoke and a foul stench rose to the heavens. (According to Rob Bell, dogs fighting over the garbage created a chaotic bedlam much like "weeping and gnashing of teeth"). No wonder first-century Jews and Christians liked to use "Gehenna" as a symbol for damnation. Gehenna is the garbage dump where the filth of humanity was thrown, unworthy of anything else.

In "The Last Word and the Word after that" Brian McLaren points out that Jesus' teachings in the gospels warn of a variety of punishments for a variety of sins. Punishment includes but is not limited to being sent to Gehenna. Listed below are some of the verses often thought to refer to eternal damnation, found in the book of Matthew. I leave it to the reader to decide which ones are actually referring to punishment in the afterlife.

Matthew 5:22-30 quite drastically warns that those who look at a woman with lust or call their brother a fool are in danger of *"the fires of Gehenna"*, and suggest that any necessary step to avoid sin, including self-mutilation, is preferable to that fate.

Matthew 7:21-22, the most ominous verses in the Bible, warn: *Not everyone who says to me, 'Lord, Lord,' will enter the kingdom of heaven, but only he who does the will of my Father who is in heaven. Many will say to me on that day, 'Lord, Lord, did we not prophesy in your name and in your name drive out demons and perform many miracles?' Then I will tell them plainly, 'I never knew you. Away from me, you evildoers!'*

Matthew 8: 10-12: *When Jesus heard this, he was astonished and said to those following him, "I tell you the truth, I have not found anyone in Israel with such great faith. I say to you that many will*

come from the east and the west, and will take their places at the feast with Abraham, Isaac and Jacob in the kingdom of heaven. But the subjects of the kingdom will be thrown outside, into the darkness, where there will be weeping and gnashing of teeth."
Matthew 12:31-32 references the mysterious unforgivable sin: *And so I tell you, every sin and blasphemy will be forgiven men, but the blasphemy against the Spirit will not be forgiven. Anyone who speaks a word against the Son of Man will be forgiven, but anyone who speaks against the Holy Spirit will not be forgiven, either in this age or in the age to come.*
Matthew 13 features several parables of judgment, where some portion of the people are thrown *"into the fiery furnace, where there is weeping and gnashing of teeth."* [13] They are distinguished as *"everything that causes sin and all who do evil"* and *"the wicked".*
Matthew 18 warns against misleading others, then repeats: *If your hand or your foot causes you to sin, cut it off and throw it away. It is better for you to enter life maimed or crippled than to have two hands or two feet and be thrown into eternal fire."* [14] It also features the parable of the ungrateful servant, where a king forgives a servant his debt. The servant is then unmerciful to a man who owes him money, and the enraged king throws the servant into debtor's prison until he pays off his debt. The parable ends with a warning: *"This is how my heavenly Father will treat each of you unless you forgive your brother from your heart."*[15]
Matthew 22 features several parables where people invited to the king's party refuse to show up. Enraged, the king invites the people on the street corners instead, *"both good and bad"*. When a man shows up without a wedding gown the king is not impressed: *"the king told the attendants, 'Tie him hand and foot, and throw him outside, into the darkness, where there will be weeping and gnashing of teeth.' For many are invited, but few are chosen."*[16]
Matthew 23 features an extended diatribe by Jesus against the cruel, hypocritical Pharisees, who manipulate God's laws and mistreat God's prophet. It includes the rhetorical question: *How will you escape the judgment of hell?*[17]
The parables of Matthew 25 teach the exclusion of those that are unprepared, and those that are lazy with their talents. The lazy

servant is likewise thrown into outer darkness.

Matthew 25, the parable of the sheep and the goats, will be discussed in detail later on. It is often considered the principal proof texts for hell, which it describes as the *"fire created for the devil and his demons"*[18] and *"eternal punishment.*[19]*"*

I will not attempt to interpret and explain all the instances of judgment mentioned above, mostly because I am unable to. It should be quite clear, however, that the actions and consequences Matthew describes do not conform to the simple "Christian = heaven, non Christian = hell" formula of modern evangelical Christianity. We will study this problem in a further chapter; for now, it simply confirms that the Biblical doctrine of hell is worthy of close examination.

What is Hell like?

Chapter 3

Author: Dante Alighieri in "The Divine Comedy"
Setting: The Juddeco, the final circle of hell, where Satan is entrapped in ice
Narrator: Dante, exploring hell

O, what a marvel it appeared to me,
  When I beheld three faces on his head!
  The one in front, and that vermilion was;
two were the others, that were joined with this
  Above the middle part of either shoulder,
  And they were joined together at the crest;
And the right-hand one seemed 'twixt white and yellow;
  The left was such to look upon as those
  Who come from where the Nile falls valley-ward.
Underneath each came forth two mighty wings,
  Such as befitting were so great a bird;
  Sails of the sea I never saw so large.
No feathers had they, but as of a bat
  Their fashion was; and he was waving them,
  So that three winds proceeded forth therefrom
  Thereby Cocytus wholly was congealed.
  With six eyes did he weep, and down three chins
  Trickled the tear-drops and the bloody drivel.
At every mouth he with his teeth was crunching
  A sinner, in the manner of a brake,
  So that he three of them tormented thus.
To him in front the biting was as naught
  Unto the clawing, for sometimes the spine
  Utterly stripped of all the skin remained.

> *"That soul up there which has the greatest pain,"*
> *The Master said, "is Judas Iscariot;*
> *With head inside, he plies his legs without.*
> *Of the two others, who head downward are,*
> *The one who hangs from the black jowl is Brutus;*
> *See how he writhes himself, and speaks no word.*
> *And the other, who so stalwart seems, is Cassius.*
> *But night is reascending, and 'tis time*
> *That we depart, for we have seen the whole."*

What is Hell like?

Even among the firmest hell-believers, agreement rarely exists about anything more concrete than "hell is bad". Not even the most common description of damnation, "separation from God", is universally believed. The Orthodox Church teaches that it is precisely God's presence that makes the afterlife painful for those who are willfully evil. The Calvinist R.C. Sproul, argues that for the unsaved, *"their problem in hell will not be separation from God; it will be the presence of God that will torment them."* Theologians have had different conceptions of hell since before the writing of the Bible. Conservative theologian John F. Waalvord notes "*it is possible to provide almost endless quotations from the Early Fathers up to modern theologians who believe in eternal punishment and those who do not.*" While the existence of some sort of hell is accepted by most Christians, its nature is very much up for debate.

Popular culture almost universally depicts hell as an underground cavern where human beings walk through leaping flames, surrounded by devils with pitchforks. The inhabitants of hell often seem quite content, e.g. skiing in Gary Larson's "far side" comics; or are otherwise "tormented" by comical punishments, like lack of toilets in the skit featuring Rowan Atkinson as the devil. These do not reflect modern theologians' beliefs about hell so much as our culture's lackadaisical attitude towards the possibility of damnation. The descendants of very conservative North American Christians, no longer really believe in hell. It is easy to make light of a cultural relic and far harder to look at a possible destiny.

Unbelievers are not the only ones who make belief in hell look somewhat ridiculous. I had a South African friend who was firmly convinced that the literal location of hell was at the center of the earth. Heat, darkness, confinement - how could damnation occur anywhere else? I must admit I began to mock him for his belief, blaming, in my arrogance, his lack of education and scientific upbringing for such a foolish belief. However, I now realize he likely learned this from highly educated North American preachers. Bible teacher Henry H. Morris suggests. "*So far as we can tell from Scripture, the present hell is somewhere in the heart of the earth itself... To say this is not scientific, is to assume science knows much more about the earth's interior than is actually the case. The great 'pit' [hell] would only need to be about 100 miles or less in diameter to contain, with much room to spare, all the forty billion or so people who have ever lived, assuming their 'spiritual' bodies are the same size as their physical bodies.*" One wonders why "spirit bodies" would need to exist in the material world and if so, if they would occupy a set amount of space, but I digress. The "center of the Earth" is as good a guess for the physical location of hell (if such a place be found) as any. Televangelist Dr. Jack van Impe has another solution. In 2001, van Impe and his wife were awarded the Ig Nobel prize (a tongue-in-cheek award given for odd scientific discoveries) for their assertion that "*black holes fulfill all the technical requirements to be the location of Hell.*"

Most theologians today consider hell, like heaven, to be a spiritual and not a material reality. Thus, it need not exist in physical space at all. The location of hell need not be defined, indeed cannot be defined, given the present state of human knowledge. Asked if hell is a physical place, Dr. J.P. Moreland responds "*yes and no. When people die, their souls leave their bodies and they're no longer physical. The Bible says when people who are ultimately headed for hell die before Christ's return, they're separated from the presence of God but they're not in a physical place because they're not physical. In that sense hell is probably not a location but it's a real part of the universe. It's like you go through a door into another kind of existence.*" Moreland goes on to suggest that hell will become a more

definable location after the second coming of Christ.
More than the location of hell, which does not seem to matter much, I am interested in the characteristics of hell. The images of devils and flames, though de-emphasized by a large proportion of modern Christians, spring readily to mind. Our pop culture images of hell come, after all, from a long tradition of the church's fire and brimstone images of damnation, images that were, and still are, held by real theologians.

Christians holding to beliefs in a literal hell of flame tend to emphasize the horrendous physical torture one can expect to experience there. The terse phrases in scripture about a "lake of fire" are extrapolated by dark imaginations, to form horror movie images of unspeakable torment. Dante's Inferno is considered by many the classic description of hell. His nine circles of torment include violent storms, crushing weights, flaming tombs, vicious dogs, whip and sword-wielding demons, pits of human feces, and lakes of boiling pitch. In the 9th circle, traitors Brutus, Cassius and Judas Iscariot are eternally mauled by a three-headed Satan trapped (ironically) in a giant block of ice. It has been said that Dante, not Jesus, is the prime source of "knowledge" about hell, and there is truth in that statement. However, he was far from the only one to depict a hell of vivid flames. The idea of fire comes from a good source, after all: the pages of the Bible.

I should note here that I will use the phrase "the literal view" to describe the view that hell has real flames that eternally torment its inhabitants. However, I am not entirely comfortable with that phrase. I believe that those who follow this view take literally some aspects of the Biblical language (flames) but take other descriptors (such as "everlasting destruction", which seems to imply non-existence) to be metaphorical. Nor do I feel entirely comfortable calling this view the "traditional view", given that the fathers of the Reformation, Martin Luther and John Calvin, did not consider the Bible's descriptions of hellfire to be literal. The term "the strong view" of hell could also be used, but that phrase assumes that other views of hell are somehow weak. In the end, I will use the term "literal view" for lack of a better descriptor.

When the Bible refers to hellfire, the place of the damned is described as "this flame": a "furnace of fire", the "eternal fire prepared for the devil and his angels", "unquenchable fire", the place where "the worm does not die and the fire is not quenched" and the "lake of fire, burning with brimstone." The Bible refers to flame in conjunction with post-mortem punishment a possible 15 times, according to John Walvoord. It is generally assumed by literalists that the soul and resurrected body of humans will feel the pain of burning, but without being consumed. The Catholic Encyclopedia says: *How can a material fire torment demons, or human souls before the resurrection of the body? But, if our soul is so joined to the body as to be keenly sensitive to the pain of fire, why should the omnipotent God be unable to bind even pure spirits to some material substance in such a manner that they suffer a torment more or less similar to the pain of fire which the soul can feel on earth?*

Not content with merely postulating fire, demons and worms, many preachers have elaborated upon these already gruesome images. Here is simply a sampling of what preachers have imagined hell to be:

Rev. J. Furniss: *"Little child, if you go to hell there will be a devil at your side to strike you. He will go on striking you every minute for ever and ever without stopping. The first stroke will make your body as bad as the body of Job, covered, from head to foot, with sores and ulcers. The second stroke will make your body twice as bad as the body of Job. The third stroke will make your body three times as bad as the body of Job. The fourth stroke will make your body four times as bad as the body of Job. How, then, will your body be after the devil has been striking it every moment for a hundred million of years without stopping? Perhaps at this moment, seven o'clock in the evening, a child is just going into hell. Tomorrow evening, at seven o'clock, go and knock at the gates of hell and ask what the child is doing. The devils will go and look. They will come back again and say, the child is burning. Go in week and ask what the child is doing; you will get the same answer, it is burning; Go in a year and asks the same answer comes it is burning. Go in a million of years and ask the same question, the answer is just the same-it is burning. So, if you go for ever and ever, you will always get the same answer - it is burning in the fire."*

Charles Spurgeon:*"When thou diest, thy soul will be tormented alone; that will be a hell for it, but at the day of judgment thy body will join thy soul, and then thou wilt have twin hells, thy soul sweating drops of blood, and thy body suffused with agony. In fire exactly like that which we have on earth thy body will lie, asbestos-like, forever unconsumed, all thy veins roads for the feet of pain to travel on, every nerve a string on which the devil shall forever play his diabolical tune of 'Hell's Unutterable Lament.'"*

The brilliant American theologian Jonathan Edwards: possibly the most famous and eloquent of hell-fire preachers, describes the fate of the damned like this: "*The wrath of God burns against them, their damnation does not slumber; the pit is prepared, the fire is made ready, the furnace is now hot, ready to receive them; the flames do now rage and glow. The glittering sword is whet, and held over them, and the pit hath opened its mouth under them.*"

Edwards also describes the hatred God feels for them: "*The God that holds you over the pit of hell, much as one holds a spider, or some loathsome insect over the fire, abhors you, and is dreadfully provoked: his wrath towards you burns like fire; he looks upon you as worthy of nothing else, but to be cast into the fire; he is of purer eyes than to bear to have you in his sight; you are ten thousand times more abominable in his eyes, than the most hateful venomous serpent is in ours.*"

Edwards again: *The world will probably be converted into a great lake or liquid globe of fire, in which the wicked shall be overwhelmed, which will always be in tempest, in which they shall be tossed to and fro, having no rest day and night, vast waves and billows of fire continually rolling over their heads, of which they shall forever be full of a quick sense within and without; their heads, their eyes, their tongues, their hands, their feet, their loins and their vitals, shall forever be full of a flowing, melting fire, fierce enough to melt the very rocks and elements; and also, they shall eternally be full of the most quick and lively sense to feel the torments; not for one minute, not for one day, not for one age, not for two ages, not for a hundred ages, nor for ten thousand millions of ages, one after another, but forever and ever, without any end at all, and never to be delivered.*

Given its horrors, it is perhaps not surprising that the literal view of hell is today being largely replaced in many denominations by the metaphorical view. The metaphorical view is the view that the Biblical descriptors of hell are to be seen as metaphors, rather than real descriptions of what hell is like. People who hold to the metaphorical view generally accept that hell is a real, dreadful and eternal reality, but they believe that the flames, undying worms, and so on are symbolic rather than literal.

    One reason for the popularity of the metaphorical view is obvious; it lacks the vivid horror of people burning forever in literal flames. Rightly or wrongly, modern Christians such as me have difficulty stomaching the thought of God literally burning another human being forever and ever. The ethical issues of eternal torment will be considered elsewhere, but thankfully there are other good logical reasons to question the literal view. Let us examine the evidence for the metaphorical view of hell.
For one thing, hell is the prison of demons and post-mortem souls. Should we expect material flames to punish immaterial beings? There must be some level of metaphor attached to any depictions of hell; if hell consists of fire, it is a fire unlike any here on Earth, for it is a fire which burns forever without fuel and will presumably cause pain to creatures without mortal bodies. Furthermore, if the Bible describes hell in fiery terms (and it does), it also describes it in ways that are distinctly different, even incompatible, with the image of burning. Fire is certainly not the only description of the afterlife of the condemned. In fact the other common description of hell, outer darkness, is one that does not mesh well with literal flames. ("*The flames would light things up*" says J.P. Moreland pragmatically, dismissing the literal view of hell.) In the book of Matthew, Jesus describes those excluded from God's kingdom as being "*thrown outside, into the darkness, where there is weeping and gnashing of teeth.*"[20] In Jesus' parables, punishment is common but it takes many different forms. In addition to fire and darkness, evildoers are punished by having their belongings taken from them, being beaten with rods, missing out on parties, being imprisoned, being executed and being dismembered. Fire is hardly the only descriptor.

    The Epistles prefer darkness to fire as a description of hell. The book of Jude describes the ultimate punishment as "*the blackest darkness."* [21] The book of 2 Thessalonians describes the presence of God as fire, but the unbeliever's lot is (ironically) separation from that fiery God: *This will happen when the Lord Jesus is revealed from heaven in blazing fire with his powerful angels. He will punish those who do not know God and do not obey the gospel of our Lord Jesus. They will be punished with everlasting destruction and shut out from the presence of the Lord and from the majesty of his power."*[22] In addition, this verse points out that fire is a common metaphor for God's judgement in scripture, even when referring (in this case) to Jesus and angels rather than hell.

Finally, in support of the "not-real-fire" argument is one of the most ironic of all Bible verses, found in Jeremiah. It references the despicable practice of child sacrifice in the valley of Ben Hinnom, the location known in the New Testament as "Gehenna" and today translated as "hell". Jeremiah writes that *"they have built the high places of Topheth in the Valley of Ben-Hinnom to burn their sons and daughters in the fire—something I did not command, nor did it enter my mind."*[23] Does God burn his sons and daughters for eternity in the fires of Gehenna - hell? Jeremiah, at least, would be surprised to hear it.

William Crocket makes the following argument in favour of the metaphorical view: *In Jewish literature, vivid pictures of hell are given to show that God has ordained an end to wickedness. The writers do not intend their descriptions to be literal depiction of the fate of the damned, but rather warnings of coming judgement. In the Qumran texts, for example, mutually exclusive concepts like fire and darkness are used more to evoke a horrifying image than to describe a literal hell. Fire is often non-literal in Jewish writings; they use colourful language to make a point. Even the Torah was said to have been written with "black fire on white fire" (Jerusalem Talmud, Shekalim 6:1, 49d) and the tree of life was described as gold-looking "in the form of fire (2 Enoch 8:4)."*

In mainstream North American Christianity, the metaphorical view has probably eclipsed the literal fire view as the most common understanding of hell. This is a relational view of damnation where separation from God, not physical torture, is the primary source of misery. As described by the Catholic encyclopedia, the poena damni, *or pain of loss, consists in the loss of the beatific vision and in so complete a separation of all the powers of the soul from God that it cannot find in Him even the least peace and rest.* (It should be noted that the Catholic encyclopedia describes hell as a place with literal fire in addition to the pain of loss.)

In the metaphorical view, the awfulness of hell comes from banishment from the source of all love, life and goodness, while the damned human remains in his evil, hopeless condition. Theologian J.P. Moreland thinks that "*God doesn't torture people in hell... God is the most generous, loving, wonderful, attractive being in the cosmos. He has made us with free will and has made us for a purpose: to lovingly relate to him and to others. And if we fail over and over again to live for the purpose for which we were created... then God will have absolutely no choice but to give us what we've asked for all along in our lives, which is separation from him... Hell is separation or banishment from the most beautiful being in the world - God himself. It is exclusion from anything that matters, from all value, not only from God but from those who have come to know and love him.*"

Evangelist Billy Graham, one of the world's most respected Christians who spent most of his life trying to get people "saved" from hell, thinks "*the only thing I could say for sure is that hell means separation from God. We are separated from his light, from his fellowship. That is going to be hell. When it comes to a literal fire, I don't preach it because I'm not sure about it. When the Scripture uses fire concerning hell, that is possibly an illustration of how terrible it's going to be - not fire but something worse, a thirst for God that cannot be quenched.*" Even the Catholic Church, which produced many of the images of boiling cauldrons filled with sinners, may be changing its tune. Pope John Paul II pronounced that *"The images of hell that sacred Scripture presents to us must be correctly interpreted. They show the complete frustration and emptiness of life without God. Rather than a place, hell indicates the state of those who freely and definitively separate themselves from God, the source of all life and joy."*

The metaphorical view of hell is not without its problems. In fact, some critics would argue that a metaphorical view of hell poses the exact same moral issues that a more literal view does. Is non-fiery suffering really more humane than suffering in actual flames? In "Four Views on Hell", Clark Pinnock critiques William Crockett's metaphorical view: *"Is the nonliteral, everlasting, conscious suffering... equivalent or not equivalent to what tradition has said about it? Is the pain of hell of the same intensity or a less fearful intensity? If [Crockett] says it is of a less fearful intensity... he wants to take the hell out of hell... but if Crockett means that hell (though non-literal) is not less fearful, what has been gained? He is still asking us to believe that God tortures people endlessly and no less severely... though the instruments would be mental rather than physical."*

I teach deeply disturbed youth for a living. Quite often, these children will engage in self-abuse: cutting themselves, banging their heads on the wall or even biting themselves; the physical pain is more bearable for them than their emotional suffering. Likewise, the metaphorical view of hell, though it seems less barbaric, is not necessarily less painful than a hell of fire. And if we do posit a less painful hell, are we trying to evade Biblical teaching? The difficulties with hell do not disappear if the Biblical images of hell are assumed to be metaphors. Perhaps the one great advantage of the metaphorical view is its uncertainty. There is a certain humility to admitting that the afterlife is in the realm of things that we are viewing *"through a glass, darkly"*[24], without certainty as to how things will be. The Biblical imagery, disturbing and even contradictory though it may be, clearly informs us that hell is a destination we need to avoid. Fire, darkness, beatings, demons, exclusion, weeping and gnashing of teeth are all unequivocally negative images, images of the tragedy of a life without God. In the end, some Christians, who hold to the metaphorical view, continue to understand God's judgement as indescribable agony. R.C. Sproul, suggests that *"It is probable that the sinner in hell would prefer a literal lake of fire as his eternal abode to the reality of hell represented in the lake of fire image"*. Others also hold the metaphorical view, but cringe at the thought of eternal torture. *The* metaphorical view of hell teaches us that fire and brimstone is not the only legitimate way to understand the language of damnation.

The Story of Satan

Chapter 4

Author: Estelle Reuter from the book "Following God's Call - Living among the Zulus"
Setting: The rural country of Kwazulu Natal, South Africa in the 1980's
Narrator: Missionary, Louis Tschirpig

Something was different about the kraal that Louis visited. There was an oppressive air the place and he had an eerie feeling in the dark hut. It had no windows and only a little light came in through the door...
He started with a greeting and then introduced the message with a Bible verse... He had only begun, when he heard a weird grunting noise... It was very annoying and he felt distracted. The repeated noisy disruptions continued all through the message, as soon as he talked about Jesus. He felt his blood starting to boil... He concluded his message quickly and was grateful when it was over... The prayer women followed him [out of the hut] and one of them said "Evangeli (evangelist), that woman that made those noises, is possessed by an evil spirit. The demon cannot stand it when the Word of God is preached and has to disrupt. Let us gather around her and pray for her." ...They all surrounded the woman... Louis could see her face. She was looking around wildly, rolling her eyes. Her movements were jerky and her arms flailed around uncontrollably.
One after the other, the prayer women started to pray for her. After some time one of them looked at Louis and said, "We cannot pray any longer, we cannot help her; you have to pray for her now." Louis was taken aback, how should he be able to help, he had no experience. He could not cast out an evil spirit. As he

was pausing to muster up some courage he said to himself, "Of course Louis, you cannot help, but Jesus can, he is able to do anything. He is almighty and can cast out the evil spirit. He has gained the victory over the devil."

Then Louis started to pray. The possessed woman did not appreciate prayer and attacked Louis with inhuman power and attempted to strangle him. Such a small woman had incredible strength!! Louis put his hands on her shoulders and gathered all the energy he had and with all the strength in his body pushed her down. She continued to rise up again and again, trying to assault him. Louis screamed "In the name of Jesus, Satan leave her!" Instantly the woman collapsed onto the floor and out of her mouth came songs of thanksgiving, which she had learned before when she had been a Christian. Harmonious praises replaced the disrupting noises.

The Story of Satan

The story of Satan is entwined with the story of hell. Jesus calls hell the "eternal fire prepared for the devil and his demons". One is, perhaps, the cause of evil in the world, the other a final solution. In popular culture, the devil is almost always located in hell. Wearing horns and wielding a pitchfork, the wisecracking overlord is generally more comical than sinister. In theology, the picture is vastly different. Jack Van Impe says, *"Most people (including most Christians) imagine [Satan] as a little creature dressed in a red uniform, running around in a place called hell, jabbing his victims with a pitchfork. This is all a lot of mythological nonsense. Hell is the place of Satan's final doom, not his refuge."*

No clear, systematic theology of the devil is found in scripture. Even his names continuously vary: the devil, Satan, the deceiver, the serpent, the dragon, the evil one, the Morning Star (Lucifer) and the King of Tyre. Understandably, there are controversies among Biblical interpreters as to which verses actually refer to Satan, instead of, say, the actual king of the place called Tyre. Satan, like hell, is described most vividly in the Bible's apocalyptic literature, and the difference between imagery and literal descriptions are not readily apparent. What is apparent is that the devil is a mighty creature: an immense, supernatural force. Christian theologians generally describe him as an archangel, the mightiest type of angel. ("*One breath from their nostrils could wipe out our entire Universe*", thinks evangelist Paul Washer.)

Beautiful, majestic and powerful, the creature known as "Lucifer" in the book of Isaiah sins against God on account of his pride and is removed from God's glorious presence. Revelation describes the fall from heaven in the following terms. *And there was war in heaven. Michael and his angels fought against the dragon, and the dragon and his angels fought back. But he was not strong enough, and they lost their place in heaven. The great dragon was hurled down—that ancient serpent called the devil, or Satan, who leads the whole world astray. He was hurled to the earth, and his angels with him.*[25]

Thrown out of heaven, the devil begins to wage war against God in a less straightforward fashion. "*Better to reign in hell than to serve in heaven*", the poet Milton describes the rebellion. Unable to battle an omnipotent God, the devil begins instead to attack God's creation, to spread the disease of evil in a formerly perfect Universe. On a "Focus on the Family" presentation, Christian novelist Frank Peretti describes it in comical but insightful terms. *Now [Satan] is pouting. He's stewing. Stomping around on the Earth... "Boy that God, what a sour person He is! Kicks me out of heaven, just because I want to be God. I mean, who does God think He is, God? Gonna get God, gonna get him"... Of course you can't 'get' God because God isn't 'getabble'... Then he looks upon the Apple of God's eye. The joy of God's creation. He looks upon mankind...*

Satan's temptation of mankind in the book of Genesis is one of the best-known, most archetypal stories in all of literature. *Now the serpent was more crafty than any of the wild animals the LORD God had made. He said to the woman, "Did God really say, 'You must not eat from any tree in the garden'?" The woman said to the serpent, "We may eat fruit from the trees in the garden, but God did say, 'You must not eat fruit from the tree that is in the middle of the garden, and you must not touch it, or you will die'". "You will not surely die," the serpent said to the woman. "For God knows that when you eat of it your eyes will be opened, and you will be like God, knowing good and evil." When the woman saw that the fruit of the tree was good for food and pleasing to the eye, and also desirable for gaining wisdom, she took some and ate it.*[26]

By choosing to disobey God, mankind had granted Satan his first victory. It would not be the last. Scripture makes it clear that the devil is our enemy, seeking our destruction. The Bible refers to Satan as a roaring lion, searching for people to devour. Zookeeper-turned-pastor Gary Richond, in "All God's Creatures" adds that he is a mortally wounded lion. Knowing full well his imminent defeat, Satan plans to wreak all the havoc he can in the meantime. Few creatures are as terrifying as a lion on the prowl. Huge steely muscles ripple beneath its skin, and its glare is pitiless, disinterested, piercing, a killer observing a piece of meat and deciding if it is worth the trouble to take it down. A wounded lion is even worse, as told in the stories of many old-time big game hunters. It will seek to destroy until the moment it dies. Richmond says *"we know the devil to be like those persistent, stalking lions. He patiently waits for just the right moment to claim our lives. The Bible has many things to say about our tenacious adversary. Jesus tells us in John 8:44 that the devil is a murderer, he has been that from the beginning. He is a predator, feeling nothing for his prey. He is without conscience, remorse, and focused on two things: deception and murder. He tries in hundreds of ways to get his claws into us and drag us down. He waits for a moment of weakness and searches for our vulnerabilities."*

It is a terrible feeling to be in another's power. I once entered the South Africa national wrestling tournament in the unfamiliar Greco-roman style. My first opponent was a world-class athlete who picked me up straight off the mat and threw me around completely at will. My best techniques could not offer even a modicum of defense. It was a dreadful feeling, even though he was kind enough to embarrass me without causing injury. How much worse to be in the clutches of the devil, a creature with the power of an archangel and the most malicious of intentions? To believe the devil exists, to really believe it, is to believe that one of the most powerful beings in existence has made it his mission to harm humanity. One cannot help but feel a tremor of fear.

The devil also is the enemy of God. *"Evil, be thou my good"* Milton describes the devil's choice. As such, he is the enemy of all goodness. He always seeks to create pain and suffering, evil and darkness, horror, hatred and loss. God wants our happiness; the devil rejoices in our suffering. God grants us salvation; the devil tries to work for the opposite. The devil, it is generally assumed, wants human beings to go to hell. *"In the End, either the enemy [God] or [the devil] will say 'mine' of everything that exists, and in particular of every man"* explains the demon Screwtape in C.S. Lewis' book The Screwtape Letters. It seems the devil is willing to fight God Himself for the souls of mankind. Luckily for us, God backs us up.

It is unclear exactly what powers the devil does or does not have at the present time. As a mighty archangel, he could presumably destroy mankind in a moment, were he not restrained by an almighty God. Why God allows the upstart to wage war instead of simply destroying him, why he gives the devil limited- though by no means total- control over humans He loves, is a question I will not presume to answer, except to suggest that God grants supernatural beings the same freedom He grants us: the freedom to make bad choices. Under what rules this battle is fought is another open question. Clearly, it is not (in military terms) a total war; an omnipotent God would make short work of the devil if He chose to. Nor does He permit Satan to wage total war on humanity. A bizarre example of this cosmic conflict is given in the book of Job. Satan asks God for permission to destroy a man's life. Curiously, God grants his wish, while still presiding over the situation. God says, *"Behold, he is in your hand, but spare his life."*[27] Job, according to Philip Yancey knows nothing of the spiritual contest raging. Yes, he somehow wins a cosmic victory by holding on to faith. If mighty Satan wages war against puny humans, then we humans have shockingly, the power in us to strike back. This power is given to us by God. (*"I saw Satan fall like lightning from heaven"*, [28]Jesus rejoices after a successful mission's trip by disciples.) In ways I'm not sure I understand, mankind can somehow fight, and even win battles in the great spiritual war. *"The gates of Hades will not prevail against the church,"* says Jesus, predicting an upset for the ages.[29]

My grandfather Louis, a man whose word I wholeheartedly trust, was a missionary in the hill country of the South African province of Kwazulu Natal for several years. One of his many stories is found at the beginning of his chapter. For many missionaries, encounters with satanic forces were common occurrences: a very real part of their job. I will confess that, in my many visits to Africa, I have never seen a person I would describe as demon-possessed. What I see, however, I consider demon-influence, behavior in humans that can only be described as demonic. It often seems that Satan is running Africa. Who else would conceive a blood-soaked mess Rwanda, Sudan and Zimbabwe have become? Who else could conceive endless blood feuds, civil wars and genocides? This is as close to hell as we can get on earth. This is what Satan wants for humanity. This is what Satan wants for eternity.

I do not claim to understand how exactly Satan works to create hell on earth, but I can see the effects, both on television and in my day-to-day experiences. As horrible as earthly suffering is, however, it pales in comparison to the prospect of eternal suffering. This seems to be the final goal of the devil, a goal which trumps even the goal to make humans suffer now.

The Christian website Earthharvest.org suggests: *Satan's purpose is to corrupt God's creation, to make man into a degenerate brute by breaking his relationship with God. He did this in Eden, and he is doing this at present. By corrupting man's knowledge of the plan of salvation, by creating other systems of belief, by promoting the occult, by debasing man, he destroys our relationship with God. There is so much dust flying in the air that the Son cannot be seen and Satan's purpose of expanding the population of hell with the unsaved is accomplished.*

My grandfather tells stories of Zulus going to witchdoctors to be cured of illness; the demons possessing the witchdoctors are only too glad to heal temporary illnesses in exchange for men's souls. C.S. Lewis' brilliant "Screwtape Letters", written from the point of view of a demon attempting to secure a Christian's damnation, explains (note that "the Enemy" refers to God). "*Consider too what undesirable deaths occur in wartime. Men are killed in places where they knew they might be killed and to which they go, if they are at all in the Enemy's party, prepared. How much better for us if all humans died in costly nursing homes amid doctors who lie, nurses who lie, friends who lie, as we have trained them, promising life to the dying, encouraging the belief that sickness excuses every indulgence, and even, if our workers know their job, withholding all suggestion of a priest lest it should betray to the sick man his true condition!... In wartime not ever a human can believe that he is going to live forever."*

The evil in the life of a rapist, is obvious, the sentiment that he will "burn in hell" when he dies widespread. The more mundane sins that separate us from God, the temptations that Satan may use on the majority of people are less obvious, but Screwtape reminds us that if the end result is the same, it doesn't matter. *"The safest road to hell is the gradual one - the gentle slope, soft underfoot, without sudden turnings, without milestones, without signposts."*

If Satan is willing and able to drag human beings down to hell with him, this raises some interesting, and depressing, theological questions. Consider the premises:
Supernatural forces are in the business of deceiving people in order to damn them.
All those who are not Christians will end up in hell.
Conclusion: ideas that question (what one understands to be "true") Christian belief are spread by the devil, with the purpose of confusing the saved humans and leading the others to destruction. This conclusion is far-reaching. Non-Christian Religions- Hinduism, Buddhism, Islam, Mormonism, and perhaps even rival branches of Christianity are not imperfect methods for worshipping God; they are the active worship of Satan. Greg Lawrie writes *"The great ethnic faiths of India, China and Japan major in demonism, as well as the animistic religions of Africa, South America and some Islands".* A veritable smorgasbord of movements and ideas, from feminism to the Beatles to the gay rights movement to liberal Christianity are seen as aggressive ploys of Satan, meant to drag more people into hell.

Furthermore, because of Satan's tremendous power and influence, nothing is safe from his poison. Nothing can be trusted; no source is so solid that the devil cannot twist it to his ends. What good is scientific evidence of, say, a 6 billion year old Earth, when the minds of scientists and even their physical evidence is at the whim of the deceiver? Even supernatural signs and wonders can be faked by the side of evil. In the world of fundamentalism, there is exactly one trustworthy guide: the Bible. Writer Rebecca Brown, in her bizarre tales of spiritual warfare, chronicles visits from angels and Jesus himself, sent to support her in battle against demonic forces. Always her response is the same: support what you are saying from Scripture. (The King-James only Christians would contend that even the Bible, apart from one specific translation, is the tool of the devil.) When reasonable Christians disagree on interpretation of Scripture, as happens on a regular basis, the mudslinging really begins. An alternate interpreter of scripture, to some fundamentalists, is at best one deceived and made useless by the devil... At worst he is one of the false apostles, a very son of Satan, spoken of in 2 Corinthians: *"For such men are false apostles, deceitful workmen, masquerading as apostles of Christ. And no wonder, for Satan himself masquerades as an angel of light"*[30]

In this theology, difference of opinion is often grounds for damnation to hell. One particularly extreme website (http://www.blessedquietness.com/journal/homemake/cslewis.htm) pronounces: *"John F. Kennedy, C.S. Lewis, and Aldous Huxley all died on the same day. They all went to the same place. Kennedy went to hell because he trusted in the Roman Whore. Huxley went to hell because he trusted in himself alone and his hybrid Eastern mystic notions. And, Lewis went to hell because he invented a new god, and he ended his life a Taoist."* C.S. Lewis, who in reality died a committed Christian, would probably make many least-likely-to-end-up-in-hell lists. Such is the power of extremist belief. Disagreement cannot be permitted, because disagreement means hell.

This theological worldview calls into question not only the nature of reality, but the nature of God. If mankind is so easily deceived, if anybody honestly seeking truth may be led astray by professional tempters and thus sucked into the pit of hell, the goodness of an omnipotent God is called into question.

If Jesus has already defeated the devil, why is the devil winning the battle for souls? If this is victory, it is surely a hollow one. After 2000 years of evangelism, non-Christians still outnumber Christians worldwide. If Satan need only keep a person from explicit Christian faith to drag him down to damnation, then Satan is doing quite well, and indeed has claimed the vast majority of souls throughout history. As Christians who believe in a triumphant God, a victorious Jesus, and a devil whose power is broken, we need to ask to question: is our thinking correct? Do all those who die without explicit Christian faith really end up in hell? We must consider the pitfalls of Christian exclusivism.

The Scope of Salvation

Chapter 5

Author: C.S. Lewis from the book "The Last Battle"
Setting: Aslan's country, the "heaven" of Narnia. The protagonists have just discovered a traditional enemy, a young Calormene soldier.
Narrator: The soldier Emeth describing his experience in Aslan's country.
"So I went over much grass and many flowers and among all kinds of wholesome and delectable trees till lo! in a narrow place between two rocks there came to meet me a great Lion. The speed of him was like the ostrich, and his size as an elephant's; his hair was like pure gold and the brightness of his eyes like gold that is liquid in the furnace. He was more terrible than the Flaming Mountain of Lagour, and in beauty he surpassed all that is in the world even as the rose in bloom surpasses the dust of the desert. Then I fell at his feet and thought, 'Surely this is the hour of death, for the Lion (who is worthy of all honour) will know that I have served Tash all my days and not him. Nevertheless, it is better to see the Lion and die than to be Tisroc of the world and live and not to have seen him.'
But the Glorious One bent down his golden head and touched my forehead with his tongue and said, 'Son, thou art welcome.'
But I said, 'Alas Lord, I am no son of thine but the servant of Tash.'
 He answered, 'Child, all the service thou hast done to Tash, I account as service done to me.' Then by reasons of my great desire for wisdom and understanding, I overcame my fear and questioned the Glorious One and said, 'Lord, is it then, as the Ape said, that thou and Tash are one?'

The Lion growled so that the earth shook (but his wrath was not against me) and said, 'It is false. Not because he and I are one, but because we are opposites, I take to me the services which thou hast done to him. For I and he are of such different kinds that no service which is vile can be done to me, and none which is not vile can be done to him. Therefore if any man swear by Tash and keep his oath for the oath's sake, it is by me that he has truly sworn, though he know it not, and it is I who reward him. And if any man do a cruelty in my name, then, though he says the name Aslan, it is Tash whom he serves and by Tash his deed is accepted. Dost thou understand, Child?'
I said, 'Lord, though knowest how much I understand. But I said also (for the truth constrained me), Yet I have been seeking Tash all my days.'
'Beloved,' said the Glorious One, 'unless thy desire had been for me thou wouldst not have sought so long and so truly. For all find what they truly seek.'"

The Scope of Salvation

Ask yourself this: Do you believe the following statement? "Ted Bundy is currently enjoying heaven, while Mahatma Gandhi suffers in hell. "

Bundy, a serial killer who admitted to murdering 30 women and suspected in the deaths of up to 100, is a prime candidate for hell if one ever existed. The "burn, Bundy, burn" signs waved outside death row as the hours ticked down to his execution bore witness to the fact that society wanted him to suffer. Mahatma Gandhi, on the other hand, is generally acknowledges as one of the greatest humanitarians and moral teachers who ever lived. His attitude to even his enemies (and Gandhi had many) was taken clearly from the teachings of his greatest hero, Jesus Christ: *"It is easy enough to be friendly to one's friends. But to befriend the one who regards himself as your enemy is the quintessence of true religion."*

What possible reason, then, would there be for Christians to believe that Bundy is in heaven while Gandhi is in hell? The distinction can be found in the much quoted words of Jesus: *"I am the Way, and the Truth, and the Life, no man comes to the*

Father except through me!"[31] Gandhi was not a Christian; he never accepted Jesus as personal Saviour and indeed, was open about his reasons for not doing so. Is Gandhi then certainly in hell?

For many evangelical Christians, salvation starts and perhaps even concludes with the prayer of salvation. The prayer of salvation is the prayer uttered when a person makes the choice to follow Christ, become a Christian, and gain entrance to heaven. It is the goal of innumerable books, tracts, websites, Bible camps, sermons and crusades. A sample "prayer of salvation" is featured at the end of many Christian books and films; it is generally spoken at altar calls in churches and at Billy Graham crusades. Many pastors, speaking on an entirely different subject, throw in a prayer of salvation as an aside in their sermons, just in case some in the audience haven't said it. A typical sample from the basic, evangelism-oriented web page: http://www.godlovestheworld.com/: *"Lord Jesus, I need You. Thank You for dying on the cross for my sins. I open the door of my life and receive You as my Savior and Lord. Thank You for forgiving my sins and giving me eternal life. Take control of the throne of my life. Make me the kind of person You want me to be."*

Perhaps the first prayer of salvation is recorded in the book of Luke, on the blood-soaked hill of Calvary two thousand years ago. As the crowds look on, three men's bodies struggled for life under the blazing sun, muscles struggling against cruel nails for each and every breath. Yet even on that hill, hours away from death, the two men crucified with Jesus force enough air into their tiring lungs to have their say. The first mocks Jesus, bitterly scorning Christ for not taking him down from the cross. The second understands salvation far better, and though every breath sends shivers of pain through his body, he squeezes out the words, first to the other thief, than to the dying Christ.

"Don't you fear God," he said, *"since you are under the same sentence? We are punished justly, for we are getting what our deeds deserve. But this man has done nothing wrong."* Then he said, *"Jesus, remember me when you come into your kingdom."* Jesus answered him, *"I tell you the truth, today you*

will be with me in paradise."[32]

In the middle of the most horrid of stories comes a shining ray of hope, God's willingness to forgive. A few simple words, uttered by a dying criminal, are all Jesus needs to hear before promising a place in paradise! Little wonder the prayer of salvation is so popular. It speaks to the glorious grace of God. It says that God loves even the killers and criminals of the world, that God is literally dying to forgive.

Quite a number of murderous criminals, facing death and, perhaps, considering hell, have prayed the prayer of salvation. Dr. James Dobson, who interviewed Ted Bundy the night before his execution, records this discussion:

Dobson: There is tremendous cynicism about you on the outside, I suppose, for good reason. I'm not sure there's anything you could say that people would believe, yet you told me (and I have heard this through our mutual friend, John Tanner) that you have accepted the forgiveness of Jesus Christ and are a follower and believer in Him. Do you draw strength from that as you approach these final hours?
Bundy: I do. I can't say that being in the Valley of the Shadow of Death is something I've become all that accustomed to, and that I'm strong and nothing's bothering me. It's no fun. It gets kind of lonely, yet I have to remind myself that every one of us will go through this someday in one way or another.

If we believe as I do, that faith in Jesus Christ itself is enough to save us from the depths of hell, then Bundy qualifies. So do fellow serial killers, the Son of Sam David Berkowitz and the cannibal Jeffrey Dahmer, both of whom reportedly confessed on their deathbeds. If we truly believe that Jesus saves, without recourse to the person's prior life or deeds and that salvation is truly a gift of matchless grace, then we can expect to see Bundy, Berkowitz and Dahmer in heaven. (Max Lucado, after listing the horrendous crimes that Dahmer has committed, comments: "*Do you know what bothers me most about Jeffrey Dahmer? His conversion.*") As the most famous verse in the Bible says, *"whosoever believes in him will never perish, but have everlasting life."*[33] Even the worst of mankind is offered the grace of God. It is the very grace of God that makes the doctrine of exclusivism so troublesome.

Christian exclusivism is the belief that only those who express faith in Christ are saved; all others will go to hell when they die. It is also known as particularism. From an angry God, a hateful God, we would expect nothing less. A God of malice and hatred and spite could well be expected to cause human beings to suffer. However, a God of love and grace and patience, a God so loving he is willing to become human and suffer torture and die for mankind; a God so filled with grace he will forgive a hardened criminal at a simple request; will this God cast his children into hell for not saying the prayer of salvation? Does this God really send people to hell because of their incorrect theology? Is everyone, absolutely everyone, who has never become a Christian, for whatever reason, really doomed?
In "A Wideness in God's mercy" Clark Pinnock suggests that the early Greek fathers were optimistic about the scope of salvation.

Take the words of Justin Martyr: "*We are taught that Christ is the first-born of God, and we have explained that he is the word of whom all mankind have had a share, and those who lived according to reason are Christians, even though they were classed as atheists. For example, among Greeks, Socrates and Heraclitus and others like him.*"

Others did not follow Martyr's optimistic view. Augustine taught narrow (exclusive) salvation and the mainstream church quickly followed. Many of the Protestant reformers disavowed much of Catholic theology, but not the belief that only a few would be saved. In fact, they turned it on the Catholics. Luther, for example, suggested that *"those who remain outside of Christianity, be they heathens, Turks, Jews or false Christians (Roman Catholics) although they believe on only one true God, yet remain in eternal wrath and perdition."*

Exclusivists are essentially pessimistic about the fate of the human race. John Calvin argued that just as Israel was a small country surrounded by unbelievers, and Noah's family formed a tiny group floating on a sea of God's destruction, so the church would form a small group of the saved amid the hell-bound masses. Did not Jesus himself state as much? The book of Matthew records: "*Enter through the narrow gate; for the gate is wide, and the way is broad that leads to destruction, and many are those who enter by it. For the gate is small, and the way is*

narrow that leads to life, and few are those who find it."[34]
Must we accept exclusivism, in which the vast majority of mankind is going to hell, as the clear teaching of Jesus? Not surprisingly, not all Christians (even those well versed in the Scriptures) agree. For a modern take on the narrow gate, a character in Brian McLaren's novel "The Last Word and the Word After That" makes the case that this does not in any way refer to the eternal destiny of people after they die. *"Jesus doesn't say the road to hell is broad; he says broad is the road to destruction... I've noticed that a lot of people tend to take anything negative - destruction, condemnation, judgment - and assume it all means hell... I don't think he says the road to heaven is narrow... It's the road to life he's talking about... Matthew [often] calls it the kingdom of heaven, but as we've discussed before, that doesn't mean "heaven after you die". It's another way of saying Kingdom of God...."* In McLaren's view, living a godly life, rather than attaining a future in a heavenly afterlife, is the point of this passage. He also suggests, along with William Barclay, that many of Jesus' warnings about destruction refer to the destruction of Jerusalem, which literally happened about 70 AD rather than about going to hell after you die. If one accepts this interpretation then it becomes clear why Matthew's gospel, written specifically to Jews, contains much more fiery and punitive language than the others.

Whether one finds McLaren's argument convincing or not, it should let us give us pause before accepting that restrictive salvation is the only truly "Christian" position. And when the **narrow road** teaching is contrasted to other statements made by Christ, (the story of the Good Shepherd who does not rest until he has found the last sheep comes to mind), we should feel free to examine the exclusivist doctrine critically. Jesus asks: *"Suppose one of you has a hundred sheep and loses one of them. Does he not leave the ninety-nine in the open country and go after the lost sheep until he finds it?"* Does God want to save the many, or only the few?

Christians often assume that the hell-bound are deliberately and knowingly rejecting God and therefore, in effect making the decision to go to hell for themselves. William Lane Craig argues: *"if we reject Christ's sacrifice for our sin, then God has no choice but to give us what we deserve. God will not send us to hell - but we will send ourselves. Our eternal destiny thus lies in our own hands.*" Yet this is not, in my opinion, self evident. I question the assumption that all those who do not "accept" Christ are willfully rejecting God's forgiveness, goodness and truth. Ravi Zacharias ensures worried Christians that: *"God himself does not send anybody to heaven or to hell; the person chooses to respond to the grace of God or to reject the grace of God".* Does it make sense for us to conclude that all human beings who are not Christians have deliberately and knowingly rejected the grace of God?

I believe that among those who do not accept the doctrines of Christianity, some do so out of honest motive: they honestly believe the Christian message to be false. My friend Jacob puts it like this: "*I do not accept that any person who is earnestly seeking to find God and find truth will ultimately become a Christian. Both from a logical point of view and from my own experiences, I do not believe that the Christian God will make himself known to anyone who really desires truth. I believe that a person of sincerity and humility of any background can end up believing in any number of religions and worldviews. I do not believe that someone who dies as a Muslim or an Atheist or a Buddhist did not become a Christian because of his or her own refusal to accept the "obvious truth" of Christianity. I cannot believe in a God who would place people in a situation where their earnest quest for truth would end with the wrong conclusions, and then damn them for it. If my only options are to burn in hell or live forever with a God like that, then it would have been better if I had never been born".*

Is Gandhi in hell? For many evangelical Christians, there is no other choice. "*Whoever believes in the Son has eternal life, but whoever rejects the Son will not see life, for God's wrath remains on him"* says the book of John, fixing in the minds of many the destiny of Gandhi. Philip Yancey reports the response he got when he wrote an article in "Christianity Today" on Gandhi, highlighting Gandhi's adherence to Jesus' teachings on nonviolence and love of neighbour. *"Although I have received plenty of venomous letters over the years, I was not prepared for the volume of hate mail the article generated. Readers informed* *me that Gandhi is now roasting in hell and that even the devil believes in God and quotes the Bible. `So it's Gandhi on the cover this month,' wrote one reader. `Who will it be next month, the Ayatollah?"*

More sensitive Christians, including Yancey himself, feel far less certain. History tells us Mahatma Gandhi loved Jesus. Gandhi loved God. What Gandhi didn't have was the belief that Jesus was the ONLY way to God. Is there hope for him? I think Christians realize instinctively that there is something wrong with rigid exclusivism. We struggle to reconcile the exclusive passages of Scripture with our real-life experiences. *"He who believes and is baptised will be saved; but he who does not believe will be condemned,"*[35] says the Gospel of Mark. *"There is no other name under heaven, given to man, through which we must be saved"*,[36] says the book of Acts. And yet we see the Dali Lama, a Buddhist, struggle for peace in a violent world. We see the largely secular Nelson Mandela, freshly released from prison, forgiving his cruel oppressors and working to reconcile with them as Christ would do. "I hope he gets himself saved", a young South African man told me. "He's my hero and I'd love to see him in heaven." We see the Gandhis of the world, people who act, for all intents and purposes, as if they have the fruits of the Spirit, and ask if God will really want to cast them aside.

Is Gandhi in hell? Ask many Christians, and you will hear uncomfortable silence. "That's all up to God", is often the answer given. (That is the answer Ravi Zacharias gives when asked in "the Case for Faith") and I have yet to come up with a better answer than that. "God will do what's right." In our heart of hearts we hope that God is more merciful, more loving, more forgiving than the theology we use to describe Him.

There are, of course, Christians, even conservative Christians, who do not believe in strict exclusivism. The alternate belief, known as Christian inclusivism, is that some people who are not professing Christians will still be saved. It is, perhaps, important to define inclusivism in the Christian sense. Christian inclusivism is not pluralism, the belief that all religions are true and valid paths to God. Nor is it universalism, the belief that all will be saved and no one will end up in hell. Inclusivism does not deny the necessity of the death of Jesus Christ for salvation. In inclusivist theology, it is still the grace of God working through the death of Jesus Christ that saves people; some of those saved may simply be ignorant of that fact. Inclusivism states that Christ can save even those with bad ideas, with wrong conceptions of God, if they are willing to be saved in some mysterious way.

Christ is the only savior - exclusivists and inclusivists alike agree. The inclusivist, however, believes that one is responsible to God for the "light" (the knowledge of Christ) that one has been given, rather than responsible to a universal standard of faith applicable to all regardless of circumstance. For those who were contemporaries of Christ, those who saw his miracles, experienced his goodness and knew witnesses who saw his resurrection, it makes perfect sense to say: *"Whoever believes in him is not condemned, but whoever does not believe stands condemned already because he has not believed in the name of God's one and only Son."*[37] Inclusivists and exclusivists alike agree that deliberate, informed rejection of Christ is a terrible thing. Yet would the same condemnation apply to a person who has never heard of Jesus Christ, or one who has been exposed to Christianity only as the religion of the conquering enemy (say, a child in present-day Iraq or Afghanistan), or one who is too mentally deficient to understand theological concepts? Rob Bell mentions a man who "*talked about Christians in his village in eastern Europe who rounded up the Muslims in town and herded them into a building where they opened fire on them with their machine guns and killed all of them*". Needless to say, this Muslim man had little interest in going to church.

Gordon Atkinson at www.realivepreacher.com records his own confrontation with the doctrine of exclusivism when a Jewish friend asks him: *"Preacher, do you think I'm going to hell?"*
I gave my polite answer. "That's really not my business. What happens to you after you die is between you and God."
That was not enough for the Rabbi who responded quickly. "No, you don't get off that easy. As I understand it, your religious tradition teaches that I will go to hell unless I accept Jesus as my savior. I don't intend to do that. I think you owe me an answer.

Do you believe I'm going to hell?"
I did not want to hear this. I'd been avoiding the subject of hell for some time, living in denial. We gentle Christians often do this. The harsh reality of our theology works against what we discover in real life. Those of us who get to know people of other faiths are profoundly moved by the experience.
"No", I said. "I do NOT believe you are going to hell. You love God more than anyone I know, more than anyone. I feel closer to you than I do to many in my own tradition. I cannot believe that about you."
He stared at me until I could look him in the eyes again and simply said, "Thank you."

Most Christians, consciously or not, allow for some inclusivism in their thinking. Not just modern Christians either. The earliest church fathers also grappled with this problem. The salvation of those who die as infants has been a classic problem in Christianity since before the time of Augustine, who famously proposed that without baptism a child who died would go to hell. John Calvin held that since the fate of a person was predestined before their birth, the "elect" children who died naturally went to heaven while the unfortunate reprobates went to hell. Today, Christians generally accept that those who die too young to hold personal faith will one day be in heaven. In "The Case for Faith", Norman Geisler argues that "*according to the Bible, every child who dies before the age of accountability goes to heaven to spend eternity in the presence of God... Isaiah 7:16 talks about an age before a child is morally accountable, before the child "knows enough to reject the wrong and choose the right". Kind David spoke of going to be with his son who died at birth. Jesus said "let the little children come to me, and do not hinder them, for the kingdom of God belongs to such as these" which indicates they will go to heaven."*[38]

Even if we consider young children who die to be safe in heaven, the problem of exclusivism does not go away. Charles Slagle sarcastically confronts the "Age of Accountability" doctrine on the web page (http://www.tentmaker.org/FAQ/DoesJesusREALLYLoveLittleChildren.html.) For the song "Jesus loves the little Children", he suggests the following revisions, simultaneously entertaining and horrifying.

"Jesus loves the world's wee children,
Until they reach the age of twelve,
Red and yellow, black and white,
Most all are doomed for darkest night,
For they will die in sin and burn in hell."

Slagle's irreverent song writing, like Atkinson's story, reminds us that doctrines of salvation and damnation are more than points to be argued about and discussed by theologians with nothing better to do. They are our understanding, flawed as it may be, of what happens to real people whom we meet and know and care for deeply. The nonbelievers we work with, the girl behind the store counter still searching for faith, the Hindu family, the quiet gay couple down the street; do we really believe that they are all doomed?

C.S. Lewis, one of the great Christian thinkers on the subject of heaven and hell, has this to say: *"The world does not consist of 100 per cent Christians and 100 per cent Non-Christians. There are people (a great many of them) who are slowly ceasing to be Christians but who still call themselves by that name: some of them are clergymen. There are other people who are slowly becoming Christians though they do not yet call themselves so. There are people who do not accept the full Christian doctrine about Christ but who are so strongly attracted by Him that they are His in a much deeper sense than they themselves understand. There are people in other religions who are being led by God's secret influence to concentrate on those parts of their religion which are in agreement with Christianity, and who thus belong to Christ without knowing it. For example, a Buddhist of good will may be led to concentrate more and more on the Buddhist teaching about mercy and to leave in the background (though he might still say he believed) the Buddhist teaching on certain other points. Many of the good Pagans long before Christ's birth may have been in this position. And always, of course, there are a great many people who are just confused in mind and have a lot of inconsistent beliefs all jumbled up together."*

If correct doctrine is necessary to go to heaven, we run

into a problem of degree. Throughout history people have tried to determine which beliefs, exactly, are necessary for salvation.

The Athanasian Creed, for example, begins with these words: *Whosoever will be saved, before all things it is necessary that he hold the catholic (i.e., universal, Christian) faith. Which faith except everyone do keep whole and undefiled, without doubt he shall perish everlastingly.* Among the doctrines this creed considers vital, the belief that Jesus "descended into hell" after his death, and that hell does indeed consist of eternal flames. Are we to assume that all those who hold to a metaphorical view of hell will be sent there? Contrast this with the Bible verse which proclaims that *"everyone who calls on the name of the Lord will be saved."*[39]

The more specific the beliefs we consider necessary for salvation, the more limited the people fulfilling that criteria. Are evangelical Christians really ready to believe that a mother Theresa, as dedicated a follower of Jesus as we may ever see, is doomed to hell for her "incorrect" Catholic faith? Once we accept that those who are not of our denomination can still access the love of God, we try to draw a line elsewhere, dismissing other Christ-followers as "cultists" who we certainly won't have to share heaven with. Which "cult" can we in good conscience exclude from the grace of God; Seventh Day Adventists, Mormons, Jehovah's Witnesses?

Finally, it goes without saying that if salvation is limited to those with an accurate theology, we need to worry about our own salvation. If God is stingy about letting people into heaven, who is to say that others are in while we are out? Let us hope, desperately hope, that God saves people based on grace, not doctrine. Otherwise, we should all be afraid.

John Wesley is hardly a theological liberal. In fact, he believed in a literal, fiery hell. Yet he, too, saw the danger in believing that people were damned for bad ideas. *"Perhaps there may be some well-meaning persons who carry this farther still; who aver, that whatever change is wrought in men, whether in their hearts or lives, yet if they have not clear views of those capital doctrines, the fall of man, justification by faith, and of the atonement made by the death of Christ, and of his righteousness transferred to them, they can have no benefit from his death. I dare in no wise affirm this. Indeed I do not believe it. I believe the merciful God regards the lives and tempers of men more than their ideas. I believe he respects the goodness of the heart rather than the clearness of the head; and that if the heart of a man be filled (by the grace of God, and the power of his Spirit) with the humble, gentle, patient love of God and man, God will not cast him into everlasting fire prepared for the devil and his angels because his ideas are not clear, or because his conceptions are confused. Without holiness, I own, "no man shall see the Lord;" but I dare not add, "or clear ideas."* In the same sermon, Wesley states his belief more succinctly: *"Nor do I conceive that any man living has a right to sentence all the heathen and Mahometan [Muslim] world to damnation. It is far better to leave them to him that made them, and who is "the Father of the spirits of all flesh;" who is the God of the Heathens as well as the Christians, and who hateth nothing that he hath made."*

Heaven and hell are, presumably, distinct (and indeed, polar opposite) destinations. At the final judgement, those who end up in hell might be easily determined from those in heaven. At present however, is not the case. Even the strong exclusivist would be hard-pressed to determine accurately among the people they know those who are really "saved" and those who are not. Jesus himself expressed that notion in the parable of the wheat and the tares, in which the righteous and the wicked are compared to crops sown in the ground, mixed with "tares" sown by an enemy. *"The servant said to [the owner of the field], 'Do you want us to go and gather them up?' But he said 'No, lest while you gather up the tares you also uproot the wheat with them. Let both grow together until the time of harvest and I will say to the reapers, 'First gather together the tares, and bind them in bundles to burn them. But gather the wheat into my barn.'"* Upon request, Jesus then explained his parable: *"The one who sowed the good seed is the Son of Man. The field is the world, and the good seed stands for the sons of the kingdom. The weeds are the sons of the evil one, and the enemy who sows them is the devil. The harvest is the end of the age, and the harvesters are angels. As the weeds are pulled up and burned in the fire, so it will be at the end of the age. The Son of Man will send out his angels, and they will weed out of his kingdom everything that causes sin and all who do evil. They will throw them into the fiery furnace, where there will be weeping and gnashing of teeth. Then the righteous will shine like the sun in the kingdom of their Father."* [40]

Jesus describes two very distinct destinies, one for the "sons of the kingdom" and another for "the sons of the evil one." However, he likewise affirms that it is not our job to do the sorting. One day, the evil will be weeded out, and those who will not follow Jesus, will weep and gnash their teeth at the coming judgement. However, until that time it would be foolish for us try and determine with certainty, which person is in and who is out. We are simply incapable of doing so, and if we attempt to do so, we risk "pulling up the wheat", condemning those already right with God.

A somewhat surprising supporter of inclusivism, given that he has spent his life convincing people it is necessary to accept Christ, is Billy Graham. Consider this interview with Robert Schuller.

Graham: [God is] calling people out of the world for His name, whether they come from the Muslim world, or the Buddhist world, or the Christian world or the non-believing world, they are members of the Body of Christ because they've been called by God. They may not even know the name of Jesus but they know in their hearts that they need something that they don't have, and they turn to the only light that they have, and I think that they are saved, and that they're going to be with us in heaven.
Schuller: What, I hear you saying that it's possible for Jesus Christ to come into human hearts and soul and life, even if they've been born in darkness and have never had exposure to the Bible. Is that a correct interpretation of what you're saying?
Graham: Yes, it is, because I believe that. I've met people in various parts of the world in tribal situations, that have never seen a Bible or heard about a Bible, and never heard of Jesus, but they've believed in their hearts that there was a God, and they've tried to live a life that was quite apart from the surrounding community in which they lived.
Schuller: I'm so thrilled to hear you say this. There's a wideness in God's mercy.
Graham: Yes, there definitely is.

One of the recent cultural phenomena in the Christian world was the response to popular pastor Rob Bell's book "Love Wins." This short book questions among other things, eternal torment and exclusivism. Bell offers more questions than answers, and his speculative theology is hardly unique, often following that of C.S. Lewis and Brian McLaren. Still yet he has received an enormous backlash from more conservative Christians. Even before the book was published, it received a massive response based on promotions alone. Influential Calvinist John Piper famously used his twitter account to bid Rob Bell goodbye. After the book was published, several books were written specifically to debunk it. Christian inclusivism is becoming a hugely popular notion. Pope Francis, who has suggested that even atheists can be redeemed and that it is not our place to judge homosexuals, has been a media sensation and was named Time Magazine's Man of the Year. The world hungers, it seems, for a more inclusive doctrine of grace.

However, it goes without saying that a more comforting belief is not necessarily a biblical or a true one. Many Catholics and Protestants alike condemn Billy Graham, Rob Bell and Pope Francis as teachers of a sentimental apostasy. Does their gentle theology have biblical backing? Let us look for biblical examples for inclusivism.

When reviewing the synoptic gospels for Jesus' teaching on hell, incorrect belief is rarely mentioned as criteria for being sent to Gehenna or Hades (as shown in the verses from Matthew's Gospel displayed earlier). While the gospel of John does emphasize the importance of faith, Matthew is more concerned with right living in the kingdom of God. Matthew's "heretical" deviations from the formula are clearest in the parable of the sheep and the goats, arguably Jesus' most straightforward teaching on the final judgment.

Many conservative Christians approach this story in an interesting manner. The description of the goat's demise is to be taken literally as a proof text for a certain vision of hell - fire, demons, endless punishment. The reason given for their punishment is largely ignored. The most obvious interpretation - that our treatment of the less fortunate determines our eternal destiny - is left untouched, for it does not fit our theology. This chapter should give warning to all of us; it should remind us that the followers of Christ are meant to live a certain way, and that simply professing loyalty to Jesus is not the only requirement of faith. At the same time, the parable contains hope for those "good" non-Christians such as Gandhi. Surely, Gandhi meets the Matthew 25 test better than most of the world's Christians. Even John, the apostle who emphasizes the importance of faith, makes the rather shocking statement that "Everyone who loves has been born of God and knows God. Whoever does not love does not know God, because God is love." Note the emphasis on love, rather than correct belief.

Furthermore, the Bible lets an obvious and significant number of non-Christians into heaven namely Old Testament heroes. The Old Testament does not focus on the afterlife. The lavish promises and fearsome threats of the Hebrew Scriptures center on this present life, rather than of heaven or hell. It is the New Testament which promises that the heroes of Scripture are safely present in heaven. The book of Hebrews praises the faith of Abel, Enoch,(who gets "taken from this life, so that he did not experience death; he could not be found, because God had taken him away"), Noah, Abraham, Moses, and so on. Yet consider that none of these patriarchs knew the name of Jesus. Some of them may have had some vague idea of a savior to come, but none of them ever said anything approximating the prayer of salvation. And yet, the writer of Hebrews 11 mentions "faith" 20 times in the chapter, just to ensure that the reader gets the hint.

Furthermore, consider the suspect "faith" of the heroes to come: Joshua, Rahab, Gideon, Barak, Samson, Jephthah and David and Samuel. The faith of Joshua and David is well-known to Christians, despite (or perhaps because of) their troubling tendency to wipe out entire nations. The others should give any reader pause.

Gideon is a reluctant, doubt-filled warrior, who celebrates his God-given victory by erecting temples to idols and beating his political rivals with thorns. Barak is another Hebrew warlord whose lack of trust annoys prophetess Deborah, not to mention God. Samson lives a depraved life, flaunting God's laws while enjoying God's gift of strength. Samson's redemption involves

one of the least Christ-like prayers in the Bible: *"O Lord God, remember me, I pray thee, and strengthen me, I pray thee, only this once, O God, that I may be at once avenged of the Philistines for my two eyes."*[41] He then pulls down a temple on himself, killing thousands of his enemies, being more suicide bomber than gentle martyr. Jephthah, yet another Old Testament warrior, has such a deficient understanding of God, that he promises to sacrifice the first thing he sees if God will hand him victory. He then sees his only daughter, and sacrifices her to God. A group of people further removed from modern (or even ancient) Christian beliefs and actions is hard to find, and yet God saves them all because their faith, flawed and sporadic as it is.
Nor is this mercy reserved for Israelites. Hebrews mentions Rahab, a career prostitute, a Canaanite woman whose tribe is so wicked that God wanted them destroyed. Rahab's redeeming act of faith was saving Joshua's spies by lying. Other non-Israelites that are, presumably in heaven include Melchizedek, priest of Salem and the unfortunate Job.

    Most Christian inclusivists will refuse to draw their own line in the sand, recognize that God alone is judge and that we can't know exactly who will be forgiven or who will not. The Christian inclusivist draws comfort from the infinite goodness and justice of God, and from God's willingness to meet people where they are and according to what they were given. As Paul records in Romans 2:

    "But because of your stubbornness and your unrepentant heart, you are storing up wrath against yourself for the day of God's wrath, when his righteous judgment will be revealed. God will give to each person according to what he has done. To those who by persistence in doing good seek glory, honor and immortality, he will give eternal life. But for those who are self-seeking and who reject the truth and follow evil, there will be wrath and anger. There will be trouble and distress for every human being who does evil: first for the Jew, then for the Gentile; but glory, honor and peace for everyone who does good: first for the Jew, then for the Gentile. For God does not show favoritism."[42]

    The Catholic theologian Karl Rahner was adamant that some non-Christians would be saved, calling them "anonymous

Christians." "Anonymous Christianity means that a person lives in the grace of God and attains salvation outside of explicitly constituted Christianity... Let us say, a Buddhist monk... who, because he follows his conscience, attains salvation and lives in the grace of God." Indeed the Catholic Church, often criticized for its hard-line conservatism and inflexibility, is generally more open to inclusivism than evangelical churches are. The old Catholic dogma that "outside the church there is no salvation" is no longer interpreted in an exclusivist way by many Catholics. The online Catholic Encyclopedia has this to say: *"the gentle breathing of grace is not confined within the walls of the Catholic Church, but reaches the hearts of many who stand afar, working in them the marvel of justification and thus ensuring the eternal salvation of numberless men who either, like upright Jews and pagans, do not know the true Church, or, like so many Protestants educated in gross prejudice, cannot appreciate her true nature. To all such, the Church does not close the gate of Heaven."* (Pope Francis goes even further. Pushing the boundaries for inclusivism in the Catholic Church, he has recently stated that well-meaning non Christians and atheists could have access to heaven.)

A protestant such as myself does not readily accept that I am "educated in gross prejudice", but I readily affirm the underlying principle behind that statement: the grace of God, not the correct understanding of theology, is where salvation lies. I am also thankful that if the Catholics turn out to be correct in their understanding of Christianity, I will not be thrown into their hell.

I do not know how far the grace of God extends, or how it applies to Indian Hindus or Iraqi Muslims or jaded Canadian agnostics, but I can take solace in the words of St. Peter, talking about the not-yet-Christian Cornelius in an unevangelized world: *'In truth I perceive that God shows no partiality, but, in every nation, whoever fears Him and works righteousness is accepted by Him."*[43]

It is frustrating but necessary that, like the nature of hell itself, the scope of salvation remains mysterious. Even Jesus' disciples tried unsuccessfully to uncover a definite answer. The book of Luke records that Jesus himself was directly about how many will be saved. Instead of a clear number, he told a story, one which emphasized both the possibility of being excluded from God's kingdom, and exhibits truly global scope of that kingdom.

"And someone said to him, "Lord, will those who are saved be few?" And he said to them, 'Strive to enter through the narrow door. For many, I tell you, will seek to enter and will not be able. When once the master of the house has risen and shut the door, and you begin to stand outside and to knock at the door, saying, 'Lord, open to us,' then he will answer you, 'I do not know where you come from.' Then you will begin to say, 'We ate and drank in your presence, and you taught in our streets.' But he will say, 'I tell you, I do not know where you come from. Depart from me, all you workers of evil!' In that place there will be weeping and gnashing of teeth, when you see Abraham and Isaac and Jacob and all the prophets in the kingdom of God but you yourselves cast out. And people will come from east and west, and from north and south, and recline at table in the kingdom of God. And behold, some are last who will be first, and some are first who will be last.'"[44]

This story, told to Jewish listeners, neatly inverts their own worldview. Confident that they were the chosen of God and those outside were not, Jesus seems to challenge them: be sure of your own salvation, and leave the rest to God. (It is also worth noting that, at the time of Jesus, people from the "east, west, north and south" had never even heard of the biblical God.)

On another occasion, Jesus again evades the question (who then can be saved?) by answering with a great biblical truth: "*With man this is impossible, but with God all things are possible.*"[45]

Let us hope and pray that it is God's will to save many, for then it will certainly come to pass.

God's Justice

Chapter 6

Author: Andrew Kaplan in the spy novel "The Scorpion"
Setting: KGB officials in cold-war era Afghanistan, torturing an Afghan for information.

With a sigh [the Russian] turned back and motioned to his men. Once again they took the red-hot iron from the coals and held it to the old man's feet, the skin long since burned to a blackened crisp.
The old man's thin scream pierced the silent hut. His breathing was labored. He was going, Mayokovsky thought.
He leaned down to the old man's ear. A fly buzzed his cheek as he did so and he irritably brushed it away. "Tell me where the Scorpion is and I'll make the pain go away," Mayakovsky whispered seductively. The old man's eyes were half-closed. Mayakovsky wasn't sure he had heard him,
But the old man had heard. His pain would be over soon, he knew. Soon Allah would gather him into his bosom and he would drink the cool waters of the Fount of Selsabil. What a fool this Russian was, he thought. As if anyone could reveal the Scorpion's whereabouts. The Scorpion was as the desert winds. The old man smiled.
Who can capture the wind?

God's Justice

Throughout Christian history, believers have struggled to cope with the apparent unfairness of God providing only two destinations - one glorious, one horrible, as reward or punishment for the vast spectrum of differently moral or immoral humans. The Roman Catholic Church attempted to solve this dilemma by introducing additional "states": those of purgatory and limbo.

Zachary Hayes argues this way: *"most of us do not die as giants of faith. Therefore, it is unlikely that we shall immediately share the destiny of the heroic martyrs of faith"* and again that ... *"therefore some sort of a cleaning process is postulated between death and the entrance into heaven".*

Purgatory may be thought of as a hellish pre-heaven state, a cleansing chamber for those who had been saved but were unfit (because of their sin) to enter heaven. Those of us who associate purgatory mainly with the abuses of the Catholic Church, Pre-Reformation, might benefit from reading the words of C.S. Lewis, who provides his interpretation of the doctrine.

"Our souls demand purgatory, don't they? Would it not break the heart if God said to us, 'It is true, my son, that your breath smells and your rags drip with mud and slime, but we are charitable here and no one will upbraid you with these things, nor draw away from you. Enter into the joy'? Should we not reply, 'With submission, sir, and if there is no objection, I'd rather be cleaned first.' 'It may hurt, you know' - 'Even so, sir.' I assume that the process of purification will normally involve suffering. Partly from tradition; partly because most real good that has been done me in this life has involved it. But I don't think the suffering is the purpose of the purgation. I can well believe that people neither much worse nor much better than I will suffer less than I or more... The treatment given will be the one required, whether it hurts little or much."

Limbo, on the other hand, has been postulated as a punishment-free section of hell. It is a place for those who were unsaved for no fault of their own, particularly those who died in infancy and the "good Pagans" who lived moral lives without ever getting a chance to hear the gospel. Limbo is, in essence, an alternate theory to inclusivism. In Limbo, souls sorrow because they are removed from God's presence, but no additional punishment is inflicted on them, their stay may indeed be quite pleasant. In Dante's Inferno "Limbo" rather resembles the Pagan version of heaven and Dante's guide Virgil (who never got the chance to meet Christ) is stationed there. In this worldview, good

Pagans don't go to heaven, but they don't burn in the lake of fire either.

The notions of a "less pleasant heaven" and a "more pleasant hell" for those who are neither great saints nor spectacular sinners have a certain common-sense appeal to them, but they have been largely rejected by Protestants, who believe rather in an all-or-nothing approach to salvation. Protestant theology emphasizes rather the all-encompassing grace of God for believers, which washes away sin so completely that there is no need for purgatorial refinement after death. Nonetheless, evangelical theologians still, in different words, admit that the experiences of salvation or damnation will be different for individuals, based on their earthly choices. We call it "loss of rewards" and "levels of punishment", but the underlying concept is the same: hell (and heaven) are not the same for everyone. *"What we do in life, echoes in eternity"* states the hero of the popular movie Gladiator, words that the Christian would do well to reflect on.

Sometimes the Bible emphasizes the extreme distinction between salvation and lostness; the glory awaiting those in the Book of Life and the sorrow of those in the Lake of Fire. At other times, the Bible speaks more about a literal judgement, a "life review", in which every word, thought and deed is measured and consequences poured out accordingly. The Apostle's Creed reminds us that Christ *"will come again to judge the living and the dead"*, a judgement that no one can avoid, whether we are "saved" or not. Our understanding of judgement needs to accommodate both the incredible grace of God, who takes on Himself the punishment for sin, so that His children need not face it; and the accountability that each person, those destined for heaven and those destined for hell, has before a fair and righteous judge.

The Bible speaks often about God holding people accountable, both those who will enter heaven and those who will not. The Apostle Paul, the great advocate of salvation by grace alone, warns a Christian audience: *"For we must all appear before the judgment seat of Christ, that each one may receive what is due him for the things done while in the body, whether good or bad."* [46] Paul goes on to paint a picture that seems positively purgatorial: *"Each one should be careful how he builds. For no one can lay any foundation other than the one already laid, which is Jesus Christ. If any man builds on this foundation using gold, silver, costly stones, wood, hay or straw, his work will be shown for what it is, because the Day will bring it to light. It will be revealed with fire, and the fire will test the quality of each man's work. If what he has built survives, he will receive his reward. If it is burned up, he will suffer loss; he himself will be saved, but only as one escaping through the flames."*[47]

For those who are enemies of Christ, judgment is likewise based on both action and circumstance. Frustrated with the obstinacy around him, an angry Jesus declares that local towns will have a less tolerable time at the last judgment than famous sinners of Sodom, Tyre and Sidon because of their blatant Christ-rejection. Jesus also tells a parable that drives home the same point: *"And that slave who knew his master's will and did not get ready or act in accord with his will, will receive many lashes but the one who did not know it, and committed deeds worthy of a flogging, will receive but few."* [48] Even Hell is subject to the laws of cause and effect. Hell is the ultimate karma.

If we accept, then, that each person in hell will be fairly punished for their actions, that hell is an earned rather than a sadistically inflicted penalty, can we accept that the eternal torment traditionally associated with hell is a just punishment? It boggles the mind that eternal torment for any human being could be considered justice.

In Biblical and Medieval times, when torture was a socially accepted punishment for crime, one might conceive of a God who also tortures His enemies. In our modern times, the pendulum has swung in the other direction, possibly too far. Many people frown on inflicting any sort of physical pain as punishment, even in the most drastic of circumstances. Spanking a disobedient child is highly controversial. Capital punishment faces legal challenges on the basis that getting killed is painful. The United States government (correctly) faces criticism over its decision to subject prisoners of war to tortures that would seem tame to medieval inquisitors. Our society is appalled by the infliction of physical pain. Little wonder, then, that the thought of God torturing sinners is barbaric to us.

Any doctrine of hell must posit that hell is an unpleasant place; were it not so, it would not be hell! Punishment, destruction and "weeping and gnashing of teeth" are common descriptions. However, the Bible itself is surprisingly sparse when talking about actual torture in hell. The Bible directly links the afterlife with "torment" a total of five times. Let us examine each instance.

The story of the Rich Man and Lazarus in the book of Luke has two of these. The rich man, being thrown into Hades, complains that "*I am in torment in this flame*" and calling it a "*place of torment*". This is the most straightforward description of a person suffering in the afterlife that the Bible provides, from the mouth of Jesus himself. We should not take it lightly. However, it is worth noting that even conservative theologians realize that *Hades* is not exactly eternal hell, but appears to be a type of in-between place where people wait for the resurrection of the dead and the final judgement. As the book of Revelation explains it, the dead will be called out of Hades to face the White Throne judgement. If the story of the Rich Man is understood to be a literal depiction of what the afterlife is like, it still describes only a place of temporal and not everlasting torment. Of "eternal torment" there are two references in Scripture, both in the book of Revelation. .

Revelation 14 states: *"A third angel followed them and said in a loud voice: "If anyone worships the beast and his image and receives his mark on the forehead or on the hand, he, too, will drink of the wine of God's fury, which has been poured full strength into the cup of his wrath. He will be tormented with burning sulfur in the presence of the holy angels and of the Lamb. And the smoke of their torment rises forever and ever. There is no rest day or night for those who worship the beast and his image, or for anyone who receives the mark of his name."* [49] Does this verse speak about hell? Fire, brimstone, torment - all the key elements of the literal view of hell are there. John Walvoord considers this a principal proof text of eternal hell; yet does this torment actually occur in hell? The torment occurs "in the presence of the Lamb", not away from the presence of God where hell is generally pictured. Furthermore, it applies to those who have worshiped the beast and received his mark; no mention is made of the unsaved dead of history.

Later on in Revelation, the devil, the beast and the false prophet are thrown into a lake of fire, where they are *"tormented with fire and brimstone forever and ever."*[50] (The reference "forever and ever" is also in dispute, an alternate translation would read "to the ages of the ages.") Universalist writer Gary Arimault, among others, argues that this verse refers to a long but finite amount of time. At the end of Revelation, all those not in the Book of Life are also thrown into the lake of fire, but no specific mention is made of their torture. I will admit a literal understanding of these verses, as currently translated in most English Bibles, implies eternal torment in hell but it does not explicitly state that it will be so for all who are sent there. Finally, the parable of the ungrateful servant in Matthew 18 features a man being tortured. *"In anger his master turned him over to the jailers to be tortured, until he should pay back all he owed."* [51] However, if we accept that the servant's punishment is symbolic of torture in hell, the fact remains that the man is being tortured for a finite amount of time, specifically until his family works long enough to pay off his debt. Finally, the man is punished because he will not forgive others, not because he is not a Christian. This verse is hardly a proof text for eternal torture in hell, though it is a very unsettling story for those who struggle to forgive other people.

As far as straightforward Biblical teaching on post-mortem torture in the afterlife goes, there is little (though more than nothing) to go by. Torturous pain has often been seen as a logical result of living in a lake of fire. However, with the metaphorical view of hell becoming more popular, the torture motif has become less common among Christians. The image of God burning, actually burning, sinners in a chamber of torture is a difficult image for Christians to stomach. This becomes all the more difficult when we worship a God whom the Bible proclaims is Love, a God who commands us to love our enemies and do good to those who hate us.

Who can love a God who tortures? If hell were a torture chamber, says theologian Nels Ferrem *"it would make Hitler a third degree saint, and the concentration camps... picnic grounds"*. Think what it means, truly means, to believe in everlasting, agonizing torture (especially coupled with an exclusivist view). To truly believe in that type of hell means that millions of Jews, tortured in the Holocaust, will be forever begging God to bring them back to the concentration camps that are more bearable than their current condition. It means that thousands of Vietnamese, burned to a crisp by the napalm drops of the Vietnam War, will never cease their agonizing screams. It means the Crusaders, as they rode through the holy land hacking and slashing and burning, were carrying out in far diluted measure what God will carry out forever and ever and ever. No wonder the literal view of hell sticks in our throats. No wonder we struggle to preach, and to believe, really believe, that the God we love will justly carry out such punishments. How many of us would feel comfortable reading the words of Jonathan Edwards from a pulpit? Can we worship the God who tortures out of anything other than fear? Can we love this God, truly love Him, instead of simply following Him in the hope that we will not be cast into the lake of fire ourselves?

Theologian Clark H. Pinnock suggests this emotional response is what produces the unwillingness of preachers to speak on the subject of hell. "*Their reticence is not so much due to a lack of integrity for proclaiming the truth as to not having the stomach for preaching a doctrine that amounts to sadism raised to new levels of finesse. Something inside tells them, perhaps on an instinctual level, that the God and Father of our Lord Jesus Christ is not the kind of deity who tortures people (even the worst of sinners) in this way.*" Brian McLaren echoes similar sentiments: "*no wonder so many theologians and preachers like myself have downplayed or entirely dropped the idea of hell in our teaching and writing. Perhaps intuitively, we have known that something is wrong and so we've backed out until we figure out the problem, or until some foolhardy person ventures to do so for us."*

Many Christians have abandoned the "physical torture" theory of hell, but cling to the belief that the suffering of hell is dreadful and eternal. William Crockett, for example, argues that *"hell should not be pictured as an inferno belching fire"* but quickly adds that *"the rebellious will be cast from the presence of*

God, without any hope of restoration... they will be driven away, but this time into "eternal night", where joy and hope are forever lost."

Eternal punishment, even if it does not qualify as physical torture, poses moral problems. My friend, Jacob, articulates the problem far better than I could:

"I fully understand that I am an imperfect creature, both by nature (which is not my doing, and for which I am not deserving of punishment) and continual choice (for which I do deserve punishment). I recognize that I do not deserve to stand before a holy God because of my willful unholiness. But do I deserve infinite punishment for my finite sin?

The first thing we have to get out of the way is the idea that some people deserve eternal torment and others don't. If there were any relationship between the degree of sin and the degree of punishment, no one could possibly deserve infinite punishment. As creatures with finite wills and powers, living finite lives in finite worlds, we cannot do infinite evil. So either Hitler does not deserve eternal suffering, or you and I and Mother Teresa all deserve it as well. If we believe in eternal punishment we must sever the intuitive link between the severity of a crime and the severity of its punishment."

Many Christians shudder at the thought of eternal hell, but see no other alternative because they believe the doctrine to be taught in scripture. In addition to the verses in Matthew 25 and Revelation, presented earlier, the Bible describes Gehenna as *"the fire that shall never be quenched"*[52] twice in the book of Mark, *"eternal destruction"*[53] in the book of Thessalonians, and also in Jude, which explains that in *"a similar way, Sodom and Gomorrah and the surrounding towns gave themselves up to sexual immorality and perversion. They serve as an example of those who suffer the punishment of eternal fire."*[54]

(Critics of the doctrine of eternal hell will note that the "eternal fire" of Sodom and Gomorrah did not, in fact, burn forever. The writer of harvestherald.com has this to say: *"Careful examination shows that the scriptures make many references to 'unquenchable fires'. But what may surprise you is that many of these 'unquenchable fires' are no longer burning. For example:*

"Therefore thus saith the Lord GOD; Behold, mine anger and my fury shall be poured out upon this place, upon man, and upon beast, and upon the trees of the field, and upon the fruit of the ground; and it shall burn, and shall not be quenched"… But did the fury and the fires spoken of here last for all eternity? Absolutely not". An unquenchable fire, in that author's view, is more akin to an unstoppable fire, one that will certainly accomplish its purpose, than a fire that will continue forever.)

Many theodicies have been written in an effort to explain how finite human sin can justly warrant infinite punishment. St. Augustine was one of the most influential defenders of an eternal hell. In a 5th century world rife with many different ideas about the fate of the unsaved, Augustine developed and defended the "eternal punishment" view that would become the predominant church teaching in the centuries to come. St. Augustine argued that any sin was a crime against an infinitely majestic God, and thus deserved an infinite punishment. This argument has been supported by theologians through the centuries, from St. Anselm to Jonathan Edwards, who explains: *"God is a being infinitely lovely, because he hath infinite excellency and beauty…so sin against God, being a violation of infinite obligations, must be a crime infinitely heinous, and so deserving infinite punishment."* For a modern example, John Walvoord: *"the problem [with people questioning eternal hell] is the obvious lack of understanding of the infinite nature of sin as contrasted to the infinite righteousness of God. If the slightest sin is infinite in its significance, then it also demands infinite punishment as a divine judgment."*

    I find this metaphysical argument hard to understand. Certainly it is an extra-Biblical argument. The Bible never provides a defense for the doctrine of eternal punishment. Eternal punishment for temporary crimes, no matter whom they are committed against, seems to me like overkill. Clark Pinnock agrees: *"Consider the Old Testament standard of justice, the standard of strict equivalence: An eye for an eye and a tooth for a tooth. Did the sinner visit upon God everlasting torment? Did he cause God or his neighbor's everlasting pain and loss? Of course not…"* Under the harsh Old Testament law, a professional torturer might deserve a lifetime of torture as punishment, but certainly no infinite penalty. Consider God's wrath in the Old Testament: shockingly harsh by our standards, but always with the promise that His anger would not last forever, that God is slow to anger and quick to forgive. If God truly is loving, would He find satisfaction from punishing a human forever?

Others who defend eternal punishment as just, emphasize the sin of man and the disgust God must surely feel in our sinful presence. Paul Washer emphasizes the wickedness of men, the righteous disgust that God has at those who flaunt his holiness. *"If I could take every thought you've ever had... and I could put them on a video, you would run off this campus in terror because you have thought things so wicked and so perverted you could not even show them to your closest friend."* Furthermore, he suggests that *"Hitler was not an anomaly. Hitler was not a phenomenon... and Hitler was still restrained by the common grace of God. And if it were not for the common grace of God you restraining you in your unconverted state, you would make Hitler look like a choirboy."*

And yet the Bible teaches, over and over again, that God has mercy on the most despicable of people; that man's sin is no barrier to God's love. The Scripture teaches that *"love covers over a multitude of sins."*[55] If those in hell are punished for ever, with no hope of redemption, it is purely at God's pleasure that they are suffering there. The punishment does them no good. Is God really glorified by people suffering eternally? Does God really need to show his disgust for man by punishing some sinners for eternity, while at the same time rescuing others? I cannot say with certainty, but every instinct I have says "no". Does God's justice somehow demand eternal damnation, regardless of God's will or desire? Brian McLaren discusses the dangers in contrasting God's love with His justice to make a case for eternal hell. *"You have to say that God doesn't want people to go to hell, but he's forced to against his will by the mechanisms of the court or some higher abstraction called justice or something like that... He wants to forgive us, but He has to play by the rules of the court. It's the only way you can make God not seem like a monster, visiting infinite punishment on poor little finite creatures who have no choice about being born into this high-risk, no win game called life… Where did these [court] mechanisms come from- some higher, sterner Senior God above the kindly junior God? Why not worship the Senior God then… [many people] worship the Senior God, who really does enjoy inflicting punishment without mercy on some while giving mercy without judgment to others…"*

The thought that God wants people to go to hell, that he creates people who are born without choice into a sinful race and then condemns them for His own glory, is too much for me to comprehend. Calvin and Augustine and Edwards may have believed it, but I cannot. My concept of holiness can only be stretched so far. Consider, as a contrast, the model of perfection Jesus tells his followers to strive for:

"But I say to you who hear, love your enemies, do good to those who hate you, bless those who curse you, pray for those who abuse you. To one who strikes you on the cheek, offer the other also, and from one who takes away your cloak do not withhold your tunic either. Give to everyone who begs from you, and from one who takes away your goods, do not demand them back. And as you wish that others would do to you, do so to them." [56]

"If you love those who love you, what benefit is that to you? For even sinners love those who love them. And if you do good to those who do good to you, what benefit is that to you? For even sinners do the same. And if you lend to those from whom you expect to receive, what credit is that to you? Even sinners lend to sinners, to get back the same amount. But love your enemies, and do good, and lend expecting nothing in return, and your reward will be great, and you will be sons of the Most High, for he is kind to the ungrateful and the evil. Be merciful, even as your Father is merciful."

Note how explicitly Christ links mercy to the evildoer with God's own character. And again: *"You have heard that it was said, 'Love your neighbor and hate your enemy". But I tell you: Love your enemies and pray for those who persecute you, that you may be sons of your Father in heaven. He causes his sun to rise on the evil and the good, and sends rain on the righteous and the unrighteous. If you love those who love you, what reward will you get? Are not even the tax collectors doing that? And if you greet only your brothers, what are you doing more than others? Do not even pagans do that? Be perfect, therefore, as your heavenly Father is perfect"*.[57]

Robert Ingersoll considers: *"They say that God says to me, "Forgive your enemies." I say, "I do;" but he says, "I will damn mine." God should be consistent. If he wants me to forgive my enemies he should forgive his. I am asked to forgive enemies who can hurt me. God is only asked to forgive enemies who cannot hurt him. He certainly ought to be as generous as he asks us to be."*

Hell and Other People

Chapter 7

Author: Steven Lawhead from the book "Arthur"
Setting: In Arthurian Britain, British forces prepare to ambush the Angi-Irish alliance making war against them.
Narrator: Sir Bedwyr, one of King Arthur's commanders
It was all I could do to keep from dashing in at once and attacking the unsuspecting enemy. But that was not the plan. Instead, we knelt at the edge of the pool and kindled the brands we had brought with us. This stole precious moments from the fight. Father of Light, kindle your wrath against our enemies and let it burn as brightly as the torches in our hands.
At last, when every man held a flaming brand, up I stood and cried the charge. My shout was answered by a thousand throats, and a thousand pairs of feet sprang forward as one. The startled barbarians turned to see a blazing wall of fire rushing towards them. We fired their camp as we passed through. The flames leapt high and the smoke curled black and thick...
  Upon reaching the foremost earthworks we seized the clay jars at our belts and smashed them against the timbers, spilling oil everywhere. We thrust the torches forth and held them. The oil sizzled and burst into flame. Greasy smoke billowed into the air. Curtains of shimmering flame leaped high. The smoke rolled to Heaven. Everywhere along the timbered maze work the assault was repeated, and the timbers began to burn.
  Now were the barbarian host entrapped in a maze of their own making. Battle taunts became shrieks of terror. Men plunged through the flames to the ground, and we ran among them with sword and shield, cutting them down. We had prayed for confusion, and were granted chaos. Angels and archangels bear witness, we gave the barbarians a taste of the burning Hell that

awaited them! Oh, it was terrible to see!
The disordered ranks of Angli and Irish collapsed. The Irish screamed and flew to the refuge of the forest. The Angli raged and began slashing at each other in utter hopelessness and frustration. In all, the enemy hordes behaved foolishly, for if they had simply held firm for a moment they would have seen how few we truly were, and how scant the fire.
But it has been said, and indeed proved true, that for all their ferocity and cunning, the barbarians are easily discouraged. They lack the spirit to stay the course. Let their scheme be thwarted and they surrender wildly to despair. They fall away; they die. Myrrdin says it is because they do not know how to hope, and I believe him. We had only to run shouting at them, throwing our torches into their midst and they faltered. Our simple surprise unnerved them. They yielded not to our swords, but to fear.

Hell and Other People

The obvious response to a place of eternal damnation is "I don't want to go there." One of the great positives of believing in hell is that it provides motivation to be right with God. Fire and brimstone preachers famously threaten their congregations with hell, in hopes of procuring revival. Jonathan Edwards bluntly and pragmatically stated that his graphic pictures of hell were intended to create fear in his congregation, so that they would repent. Indeed, fear is a proper response to hell . *"What does it profit any man"*, asked Jesus rhetorically, *"if he gains the world, and in the end he loses his own soul?"* [58] Edwards describes the proper and logical response for a man who fears being thrown into hell: *So distressed, that he is brought to be willing to do anything; to have salvation on any terms, and by any means, however difficult; brought, as it were, to write a blank, and give it in to God, that God may prescribe his own terms."*
The Bible is not above using the same terms: *"If your eye offends you, pluck it out"* says Jesus. *"Better to lose one eye, than have both eyes and be thrown into hell!"*[59] Brain McLaren suggests

that Jesus' sermons about hell are less theological treaties about the hereafter, than warnings to turn people away from sin. Perhaps, hell is there to create fear. Fear to believe. Fear to cause belief and good behavior. Fear to prevent people from doing horrible things to each other. *"There are times when we fall back into primitive behavior, when we want to kill somebody. If hell keeps us from doing it, I say, 'Bless hell'"* suggests a Weekly World Report about belief in hell.

In addition to fearing hell, hell makes us fear God. Jesus pragmatically suggests that instead of fearing people, *"Fear the One who after He has killed has authority to cast into hell; yes, I tell you, fear Him!"*[60] Whether this is a positive or a negative thing is an open question. Liberal Christianity, light on hellfire, risks neglecting the awesome majesty and total sovereignty of God in its teaching. Paul Washer thinks that the doctrine of hell reminds us of our creaturely status, reminds us that God is to be reckoned with and that the universe does not revolve around us. God is not there to serve us; we are there to serve God. Hell certainly puts the fear of God into us. What it does not do is give us incentive to love. Who among us could love a romantic partner that gave us a choice between a relationship and a beating? The Bible frequently portrays Jesus as romancing his Bride; the church - an image that seems downright abusive if the choice is between romance and punishment.

A belief in hell is also strong motivation to evangelize others. William MacDonald suggests that Christians *"should think about relatives, friends, neighbors, men everywhere who will soon be [in hell]. They should think about it long enough so that they will never be able to live normal, routine, complacent Christian lives again."* If others are headed for hell, it is our job to warn them. Let the heroes who have spread our faith speak, in their own words, and explain their motivation to spread the Gospel of Christ (or, as C.T. Studd says, *"run a rescue shop within a yard of hell."*)

K.P. Yohannan, the founder of Gospel for Asia Bible Society writes, *"Believers who have the gospel keep mumbling it over and over to themselves. Meanwhile, millions who have never heard it once fall into the flames of eternal hell without ever hearing the salvation story."*

William Booth, founder of Salvation Army says, *"Put your ear down to the Bible, and hear Him bid you go and pull sinners out of the fire of sin. Put your ear down to the burdened, agonized heart of humanity, and listen to its pitiful wail for help. Go stand by the gates of hell, and hear the damned entreat you to go to their father's house and bid their brothers and sisters and servants and masters not to come there. Then look Christ in the face - whose mercy you have professed to obey - and tell Him whether you will join heart and soul and body and circumstances in the march to publish His mercy to the world."*

CH Spurgeon: *"If sinners will be damned, at least let them leap to hell over our bodies. And if they will perish, let them perish with our arms around their knees, imploring them to stay. If hell must be filled, at least let it be filled in the teeth of our exertions, and let not one go there unwarned and unprayed for."*

The exclusivist Christian who truly believes that his neighbours are lost, cut off from God, and destined to hell has the greatest of motivations to introduce them to Christ. As a young man, I felt deep shame about my failure to evangelize. I was wracked with guilt when, time after time, I was too cowardly to share my faith. I felt as if every moment not spent in evangelizing my neighbour, was a moment wasted. In one of my more embarrassing moments, I told God I would evangelize a friend if he helped me to win a wrestling competition. I won and then didn't. I still wonder what God thought of the whole thing. I remember being given tickets by a shy Christian girl to attend a play called "Heaven's Gates and Hell's Flames" while I was in high school. My family and I attended, hoping for an evening of wholesome Christian entertainment, and were treated to the most blatant of manipulation tactics in the name of saving souls. One after another, characters appeared on stage and discussed the possibility of accepting Jesus as their personal Saviour. One after the other, they promptly died in poorly staged accidents and, based on their decisions, were welcomed into heaven or dragged (accompanied by flashing lights and scary music) into a fiery hell by the devil. Long before I began to seriously question my belief in hell, such blatant manipulation left a bitter taste in my mouth. Afterwards, there was an altar call, and I wondered if any of the teary-eyed people making their way to the front would get out of hell free because the play had successfully manipulated their emotions; I wondered if God could be manipulated also.

To my knowledge, my friend "Jacob" has never seen this particular play, but based on his writing he has been subjected to similar evangelization attempts. *"If souls can be saved through deception, emotional manipulation or scare tactics, how can these things be bad? ...Emotional "worship" services, spiritual parlor tricks, dishonest marketing, hidden-agenda friendships, and so forth. I once worked at a week-long children's camp where the gospel (that is, a plea to believe in Jesus and be saved from hell) was presented at every opportunity - generally about four times a day. To me, this seemed like a desperate and unscrupulous attempt to nag, scare, or brainwash small children into joining our religion. To other staff, it was taking seriously our mandate to save souls."*

Having worked with my friend at the same camp, I can attest to Jacob's words. The fear of hell was hammered into children repeatedly, sometimes around a massive campfire, where the miserable heat nicely emphasized the preacher's searing words. "I wish I could grab you and shake you and beat salvation into you, but I can't" implored one enormous man, who thankfully realized that shaking the children was crossing a moral line. Another preacher referenced a recent plane crash and asked the children to imagine the screams and the smells of burning flesh. That's what hell is like, after all. (Richard Dawkins, for one, thinks this kind of evangelism is child abuse.) A friend who went to a similar camp recounts waking up crying in the weeks to follow, terrified of hell and begging Jesus to save her. Not surprisingly, she no longer believes in hell, unable to reconcile such a place with the God she loves.

Today, I still live in unresolved tension when it comes to evangelism techniques. I admire those who smuggle Bibles past inquisitive border guards into communist countries, but disdain those who threaten children with hellfire. And yet, I cannot shake the uneasy notion that they are one and the same. If our action or inaction will save a person from the fires of hell, all other moral issues fall away. Seen in the flickering light of hell, even the actions of medieval warlords and inquisitors begin to make more sense. What is the most immoral of actions, even physical torture, if it turns a person from eternal torture? Real Live preacher gives a facetious but real-life example: *"Yes, it is believed that even a young woman raised in a primitive culture in an isolated jungle will go to hell if she dies without becoming a Christian. That's why we have to get missionaries over there, chop chop. To save her and others like her. True, our arrival will destroy her delicate culture and expose her people to deadly diseases and other Western things that will undoubtedly be harmful, but all other concerns pale when compared to eternal torment, do they not?"*

Philip Yancey suggests that the Bible is unclear about who exactly will end up in hell, precisely to save the world from overzealous evangelists. *"Consider infant salvation... What if God had made a clear pronouncement: "Thus saith the Lord, I will welcome every child under the age of ten into heaven." I can easily envision Crusaders of the eleventh century mounting a campaign to slaughter every child of nine or younger in order to guarantee their eternal salvation- which of course means that none of us would be around a millennium later to contemplate such questions."*

Luckily, sanity has prevailed and there has been no mass slaughter of babies by Christians. Yet I remember an eerie story from my childhood, concerning a friend of my grandfather's who had the gift of healing. When he prayed for healing, things happened. A man begged the healer to pray for his child, who was deathly ill. The healer considered. "I can, if you want me to", he said "but let me warn you that if the child dies now, he will be saved and enter heaven. If he recovers and lives a long life, who knows?" Both father and healer decided it would be better for the child to die. Real belief in hell has strange consequences.

Part of my childhood was spent in South Africa, a country known for racial tension stemming from its oppressive history of white supremacy. As far as I know, the heavily Calvinist Dutch Reformed Church (the national church of apartheid-era South Africa) never officially taught that whites are "elect" while black are "reprobate". However, the fingerprints of such thinking could be found all over the political system of Apartheid. Given that God loves and chooses some people, and despises others (as shown by His willingness to predestine them to hell), it is easy to decide that one's social or political enemies are the reprobate, despised by God Himself and thus worthy of inferior treatment. For fifty years, the deeply Christian Afrikaners found themselves supporting a political system that treated whites as the chosen and blacks as the outcast peoples, supported wholeheartedly by the Dutch Reformed church.

Today, many homosexuals are subject to the same treatment. The infamous Westboro Baptist Church teaches a hell-based theology taken to extremes. Reverend Fred Phelp's radical anti-homosexual message (the church's website is www.godhatesfags.com) is disavowed by mainstream churches, Baptist or otherwise, and he is alleged to be mentally ill. Nevertheless, his straightforward approach to hell should give us food for thought. When the gay Matthew Sheppard was brutally tortured and murdered, Westboro parishioners picketed the funeral, waving signs stating that "Matt rots in hell." The church set up a website with a picture of flames superimposed upon Matt's face, equipped with audio so you could hear the man screaming. The website also had a "hell-counter" which counted the number of days Mr. Sheppard had been burning, with the helpful explanation that he was there for eternity. Mr. Phelps may well be clinically insane, but it does force me to face unpleasant questions: is Matthew Sheppard really in hell? Will he really suffer there for eternity? If these things are true, how should they affect my attitude towards other people? For too many people, the answer is simple: if God hates some people, homosexual or otherwise, why shouldn't we?

The idea, twisted as it seems, that the saved should rejoice over the suffering of the damned is not new. Thomas Aquinas famously thought *"that the saints may enjoy their beatitude and the grace of God more abundantly; they are permitted to see the punishment of the damned in hell."* Tertullian was more descriptive: *" How I shall admire, how laugh, how exalt when I behold so many proud monarchs groaning in the lower abyss of darkness . . . so many sage philosophers blushing in red hot fires with their deluded pupils."* William Barclay suggests that such attitudes came about because of the horrible suffering Christian martyrs were forced to endure and their understandable desire for ultimate justice. Barclay considers such an attitude "sub-Christian" but suggests we should not judge those church fathers until we have suffered for the faith as they have.

Unfortunately, however, such thinking is not confined to persecuted church fathers. Consider lines from a hymn by Isaac Watts: *What bliss will fill the ransomed souls, When they in glory dwell, To see the sinner as he rolls, In quenchless flames of hell.* For a more modern example, consider political pundit Ann Coulter's comment that *""I defy any of my co-religionists to tell me they do not laugh at the idea of [atheist Richard] Dawkins burning in hell."*

From rejoicing in the torment of another, it is but a short step to perpetuating that torment oneself. Thomas Paine said that *"belief in a cruel God makes a cruel man"* and I think that he was right. How many of the church's atrocities throughout history can be traced back to a belief in a vengeful God, a God who delights in wrath and punishment and raining down fire on sinners? Too many Christians, motivated more by Joshua than Jesus, have seen themselves as the warriors of God, fighting against those already doomed to hell. To quote Brian McLaren: *"[hell] can create a view of God as vengeful torturer, and that has played a role, I believe, in horrible behavior on the part of Western Christians—from anti-Semitism to slavery and racism and holy-war mentality. In other words, if we can identify some people as God's enemies, hated by God for all eternity, we can find ourselves directly disobeying Jesus' clear teachings about loving our neighbors and our enemies".*

In "A History of Torture", Joseph McCabe argues that the Christians of medieval Europe used torture more than any society in history. The reason he gives? Their strong belief in hell, which taught them that God Himself tortures, and sanctions others to do the same. The English Queen "Bloody Mary" justified her government's tortures thus: *"As the souls of heretics are to be forever burning in hell, there can be nothing more proper than for me to imitate the Divine vengeance by burning them here on earth."* Just as bad was the solution of 13th century Abbot Amaud Amalric, whose army was trying to root out the heretics in a town that refused to deliver them. *"Kill them all, the Lord knows those that are his."* If the righteous went to heaven and the unrighteous to hell, why not send them all to the judgment seat of Christ and be done with it?

Conservative Christians may shudder at these words, and hasten to protest that such behavior is at odds with orthodox Christian faith. They are right, of course, but we should pause a moment and realize how doctrines of exclusivism and eternal hell can influence such behavior.

It goes without saying that most Christians do not want to torture Non-Christians, and indeed, are rightly appalled at the prospect. However, I wonder if we don't make our disdain for the "unsaved" known in more subtle ways. I once went to a Bible camp where I was met by a very friendly woman who shook my hand and asked two questions: "Do you want to go canoeing with me?" and "are you saved?" Our friendship was instantly defined by my predicted entrance to heaven or hell. When the televangelist Jerry Falwall offended many by claiming that *"If you're not a born-again Christian, you're a failure as a human being"* he was simply expressing a fundamental tenant of exclusivist theology. If you don't convert, you are of so little use to God that he will throw you on the trash pile and set it on fire. Such thinking was the norm for me throughout my childhood. I could never quite picture hell as a lake of fire; rather it was always a very dark and gloomy place in my mind, an underground cavern perhaps where the damned were depressed and alone. Looking at my classmates, I would imagine those I knew to be Christians - the saved - as real, vibrant people, while the "unsaved" were shadowy specters on their way to hell. In school, I learned about Aristotle and Socrates, and I wondered what the point was: how important could the teaching of a person condemned to hell be? The Greek philosophers seemed kind and wise, and I hoped that they weren't too uncomfortable there.

My friend, Jacob, points out that even love for others is difficult when it is likely that they will be lost forever. Christians who believe in hell must live in the terrible knowledge that many of the people they love will suffer eternally. After listening to a Focus on the Family broadcast where a Christian man mourns the death of his unsaved wife, blogger Jacob had this to say: *"It struck me that the implicit message here is, don't love non-Christians too much. Don't care too much about them. Don't feel for them too much of what God feels. Don't understand too deeply their immeasurable, inherent value, because if you do, and they die unsaved, you will see too clearly the incomparable tragedy and horror of hell, and it will break you".* I think that the death of a loved one has made many a Christian an inclusivist.

Finally, while preaching hell might drive some people to faith, it probably drives away just as many. The great missionaries of old (preaching in many cases to tribes awed by the missionaries, godlike technology and haunted by their own vengeful gods) had no trouble convincing people to accept Christ to escape eternal hell. In our own, often secular culture, preaching hell may not be the best approach to spreading faith. A modern-day missionary (whose own views on hell are conservative) recently advised me: *"people used to accept salvation to escape the judgment of hell. Now they do it to accept companionship because they are lonely."* In one of his NOOMA videos on faith, Rob Bell describes meeting an evangelist who stands on a street corner, shouting into a bullhorn. *"As I get closer I hear the words "sin" and "burn" and "hell" "repent".... And then I hear the word "Jesus"... he's got all these pamphlets and he's quoting these Bible verses about the anger and the wrath of God, and how if I don't repent, I'm gonna pay for it for eternity... And no one is stopping to hear more, and no one wants any of its pamphlets. And so I want to talk to the Bullhorn Guy. Bullhorn Guy, I don't think it's working."*

Belief in hell may scare some people into Christian faith. My sister asked me many years ago if she thought God accepted such people, who held onto faith primarily for fire insurance. "I hope so", I told her, "I'm one of them." For a lustful teenager with rebellious friends, fear of hell seemed the only reason good enough to follow the commandments of God. However, as an adult, I found that the doctrine of hell became, and still is, my single greatest hurdle towards faith in God. Hell makes me doubt God, fear God, even (in my less admirable moments) struggle not to hate God. Hell may motivate belief, but it's also great at causing unbelief. It is arguably the single greatest theological stumbling stone for would-be believers.

To read the great humanist, agnostic and atheistic thinkers

(Bertrand Russel, Charles Darwin, Richard Dawkins, Charles Templeton and Robert Ingersoll to name a few) is to read complaints about the unfairness of hell. Modern unbelievers are quite vocal about the apparent absurdities of eternal punishment, and insulted rather than terrified by the idea that they themselves might someday go there. *"I must say that I think all this doctrine, that hell-fire is a punishment for sin, is a doctrine of cruelty. It is a doctrine that put cruelty into the world and gave the world generations of cruel torture"*, wrote Russel in his famous "I am Not a Christian".

Brian McLaren's protagonist in "the Last Word and the Word After That" worries about a girl losing her faith *"... like the millions of others, young and old, who have given up on Christianity because the way we talk about God sounds absolutely wacky. 'God loves you and has a wonderful plan for your life', we say, 'and he'll fry your butt in hell forever unless you do or believe the right thing.' 'God's a loving father,' we say, 'but he'll treat you with a cruelty no human father has ever been guilty of - eternal conscious torture."* It is not just the cruelty that drives people away. We can envision a God who likes to punish- Edwards did. More difficult is simultaneously believing, as John states, *"God is Love"*. For the seeker or the unbeliever, it is not enough to explain away the apparent contradiction by stating that "the Bible says so". Far from scaring people into faith, hell theology drives many people away. Even if for no other reason than this, we must continue to grapple with and revisit our traditional notions of hell.

Finally, it needs to be asked: if a fiery hell is a traditional motivator for Christians to share their faith with others, what about those Christians who doubt the doctrine of literal, exclusivist hell? In the movie "Anne of Green Gables", the town gossip comments on a pastor's inclusive theology: *"Can you believe that new preacher going on about how he doesn't believe that all of the heathen will be eternally lost? If they won't be, all the money we are sending to missions will be completely wasted, that's what!"*

If we struggle to believe in some or all of the doctrines of exclusivism, fiery torture and unending punishment, why should we still care about spreading the gospel of Christ? I believe there are several good reasons for a Christian to share their faith, regardless of their convictions on hell.

1: Jesus commands it. Jesus' last instructions to his disciples are, *"Go into the world and make disciples of all nations"*. It is simple obedience to Jesus to evangelize others.

2: The good news about Jesus is more than so-called "fire insurance". The book of Acts, the New Testament's primary account of early missionaries, does not mention hell, and the sermons preached by its heroes are generally upbeat rather than threatening in nature. They preached the glory of Christ's resurrection, the forgiveness of sins, the presence of the kingdom of God and the invitation to join the kingdom. Christ provides so much more than escape from hell. A pastor once told me that "people are in hell now; the hell of living without God." It is our mission to bring a message of God's love, forgiveness and help to people, regardless of where they will end up after they die.

3: Evangelism, done right, should include physical and practical help. Christians are asked to minister both to the physical and spiritual needs of others. Jesus said:, *"...for I was hungry, and you gave me food to eat. I was thirsty, and you gave me drink. I was a stranger, and you took me in. I was naked, and you clothed me. I was sick, and you visited me. I was in prison, and you came to me."*[61] To be a missionary is, or rather should be, to be an agent of goodness in the world, sharing both Christ's heavenly salvation and God's kingdom here on Earth with others.

4: Finally it should be noted that those with non-literal beliefs in hell still, generally speaking, accept God's judgment as a final reality. The inclusivist does not believe that all unevangelized persons will go to hell, but neither does he believe that all unevangelized people will go to heaven. There are still the "lost" to be reached, even if we don't know exactly who is or is not "lost". Those who believe in a non-fiery hell or a temporary hell (ending in annihilation or in reconciliation) still believe that a terrible fate awaits those who reject Christ. A Christian may evangelize not only so that others will avoid eternity in a lake of literal fire, but rather that others may avoid God's wrath and judgment in whatever form it may take.

The Experience of Hell

Chapter 8

Author: Blogger "Jacob" at www.twentyfeet.blogspot.com
There was once a young man who demanded his inheritance from his father and then moved to a distant land and squandered it on parties and prostitutes. He became so poor that he could no longer feed himself, and the only job he could find was feeding pigs, for which he was payed so little that even the pig slop looked good to him.
He soon realized what a fool he'd been and remembered his father, who was a kind man and generous to his workers. He wondered if he should return home. Of course he would not ask his father to accept him as his son, but perhaps he would have mercy on him and hire him to work in his fields. But whenever he thought of his father, he was filled with shame and fear, and could not bring himself to go home.
Then one day as he was sitting in the mud with the pigs, he saw his father approaching. Fear and guilt gripped him, and he could not meet his father's eye. But his father bent down in the mud and touched him. "My son, why have you not come home?"
The son looked up, sorrowfully. "I was afraid. I was ashamed. I didn't think you'd want to see me again."
"You were wrong. Every day I've stood at my window and waited for you to come home. Even though you despised me, shamed me, turned your back on me, I have always been your father, and I have always loved you and longed to forgive you. If you had come home I would have run out to meet you. I would have given you a new robe and a ring, and I would have embraced you and kissed you and celebrated your coming with a feast. We would have rejoiced together as if you were dead and had come back to life!"

The son looked at his father in wonder. "You would do that for me? Even now you would forgive me for all I've done?"
The father shook his head. "No, I said I would have forgiven you, but I will not forgive you now. Since your birth and despite all your faults and failures I have loved you, but my love has ended. All these years you could have returned to me - even yesterday I would have embraced you as a son - but not today. I've come to tell you that on this day I disown you and I withdraw my forgiveness and my love. I am no longer your father; you are no longer my son. Do what you will - beg, starve, die in the streets. I care less for you than for these pigs, even less than for the slop you feed them or the mud you're sitting in. Whatever remorse you may now feel, however much you may long for my forgiveness, until the day you die you will never again speak with me or enter my presence."
And the father turned his back on the one who was once his son, and left him in the mud with the pigs.

The Experience of Hell

Perhaps because we lack imagination, we often imagine life on hell to be, as Deepak Chopra says, *"like life on earth, only worse"*. Other than the *"weeping and gnashing of teeth"*, there is little to go on Biblically to describe what people actually do in hell. The book of Revelation describes the character of those who are cast into the Lake of Fire: *"the fearful, the unbelieving, the abominable, and murderers, and whoremongerers, and sorcerers, and idolaters, and all liars"*... [62]Altogether an unpleasant group.

The closest thing the Bible gives to explaining the human condition in hell (or rather, Hades) is the famous "Rich Man and Lazarus" parable found in Luke. *"There was a rich man who was dressed in purple and fine linen and lived in luxury every day. At his gate was laid a beggar named Lazarus, covered with sores and longing to eat what fell from the rich man's table. Even the dogs came and licked his sores. The time came when the beggar died and the angels carried him to Abraham's side. The rich man also died and was buried. In Hades, where he was in torment, he looked up and saw Abraham far away, with Lazarus by his side. So he called to him, 'Father Abraham, have pity on me and send Lazarus to dip the tip of his finger in water and cool my tongue, because I am in agony in this fire.'*

"But Abraham replied, 'Son, remember that in your lifetime you received your good things, while Lazarus received bad things, but now he is comforted here and you are in agony. And besides all this, between us and you a great chasm has been fixed, so that those who want to go from here to you cannot, nor can anyone cross over from there to us.' "He answered, 'Then I beg you, father, send Lazarus to my father's house, for I have five brothers. Let him warn them, so that they will not also come to this place of torment.' "Abraham replied, 'They have Moses and the Prophets; let them listen to them.'" 'No, father Abraham,' he said, 'but if someone from the dead goes to them, they will repent.' "He said to him, 'If they do not listen to Moses and the Prophets, they will not be convinced even if someone rises from the dead.' "[63]

It is by no means certain that this story is meant to provide factual details of the afterlife. Biblical scholars note that it is, quite likely, a twist on a well-known "role reversal" story of Jesus day, using Jewish mythology as the backdrop. Jesus may be trying to teach important lessons about caring for the beggars at our doorstep and heeding the warnings of Scripture, rather than providing details on the afterlife. Nor should this story be read without a certain sense of irony, given that Jesus' contemporaries were in fact, provided with the witness of a man named Lazarus who was raised from the dead. Finally, it is worth remembering that Hades and the final hell are not considered the same thing by many theologians.

Nonetheless, despite these objections, and despite the fact that many details of the story do not correspond to traditional Christian understandings of the afterlife, it has long been analyzed as a literal description about hell. I note the following: The rich man retains a physical body (has eyes and a tongue). The rich man feels physical pain (*"I am in torment in this flame"*), though not so much pain that he is incapable of meaningful conversation. The rich man is separated from paradise *("there is a great gulf fixed")*. He exhibits both moral qualities (care for his brothers) and immoral ones (still looks down on Lazarus as a servant). Finally, he does not show repentance, or even a desire to leave Hades; he simply asks that his stay be made more comfortable. More strangely, he can talk to Abraham in paradise, who seems to have some administrative position!

Whether these assumptions hold true for an actual place I do not pretend to know. If we do not accept the authority of Abraham in paradise, the soul-carrying angels or the Hades/heaven conversation as literal realities about the afterlife, should we accept the conditions described in Hades as literal? None the less, we can use the parable as a starting point for interesting speculation, once again keeping in mind that Hades is a "holding cell" rather than an eternal destination in Scripture. C.S. Lewis urges caution: *"the New Testament plainly implies the possibility of some being finally left in 'the outer darkness.' Whether this means...being left to a purely mental state...or whether there is still some sort of environment, something you could call a world or a reality, I would never pretend to know".* Unlike Lewis, some other Christians have very specific ideas about the human experience in hell, and are not shy about sharing them. Erwin Lutzer, relying heavily on the "Rich Man" story, thinks that the flames of hell drive people to useless repentance, begging for mercy that will never come. The "Left Behind" series similarly presents the Antichrist and False Prophet as eternally, and pointlessly, calling out "Jesus is Lord" as they burn on their knees. Jack van Impe, on the other hand, thinks the hell-bound never repent, gnashing their teeth with hatred of God as they continue to sin. So does Max Lucado, who feels that *"death freezes the moral compass. People will remain in the fashion they enter."* Dante sees the damned reverting to a more primal, almost animal state, as does modern preacher Paul Washer, who suspects that people will become more and more evil, and less and less human, the longer they are in hell.

Most believers seem to agree that hell's inhabitants feel lonely, haunted and sad. J.P. Moreland describes a place of regret and self-loathing. *"The punishment of hell is separation from God, bringing shame, anguish, and regret... the pain that's suffered will be due to the sorrow from the ultimate, unending banishment from God, his kingdom, and the good life for which we were created in the first place. People in hell will deeply grieve all they've lost."*

Lucado describes hell as a place where people continually suffer because they are sinful: *"hell is individuals at their worst. It surfaces and amplifies the ugliest traits in people. Cravings will go unchecked. Worriers will fret and never find peace. Thieves will steal and never have enough. Drunks always craving, gluttons always demanding. None will be satisfied. Remember: "their worm does not die."*

I once asked a South African pastor to describe hell for me. He considered it for a while, and though he thought that "the Bible talks about torture" he didn't think physical pain or burning flames were important details. What mattered, he said, was the utter hopelessness. "On Earth, any human being can call out 'God help me'! In hell we no longer have that privilege. And hell will be incredibly boring, nothing to do at all."
"You shouldn't worry about that", thought his ever-practical wife. "You should worry about the worms eating your flesh!"

If hell is a place of suffering, it is either a place of bearable or a place of unbearable suffering. Living human beings, knowing with certainty that their suffering is temporary, can be driven to despair and even insanity through pain. How much more then would a person in hell, facing a prospect of unending agony, be affected mentally? This could not but help drive a person into utter madness. Ever helpful, Jonathan Edward describes that state: *"The damned in hell in their misery will be in absolute despair. They shall know that their misery will have no end, and therefore they will have no hopes of it... To what unfathomable depths of woe will it sink them! With what a gloom and blackness of darkness will it fill them."* If hell is unbearable torture (physical, emotional or both matters not) the citizens of hell would quickly become something other than human, horrible vessels whose only purpose and goal is to transmit the feeling of pain to insane minds. We cannot begin to imagine such a non-existence.

C.S. Lewis suggests that human selfishness, rather than divinely inflicted torment, serves to destroy all humanity in those in hell: *"to enter hell is to be banished from humanity. What is cast (or casts itself) into hell is not a man; it is remains. To be a complete man [in heaven] is to have the passions obedient to the will and the will offered to God: to have been a man... would presumably mean to exist as a will utterly centered in itself and passions utterly uncontrolled by the will. It is off course impossible to imagine what the consciousness of such a creature- already a loose congeries of mutually antagonistic sins rather than a sinner, would be like."*

Lewis seemed to believe that while the humanity of the hellbound would be destroyed, some spark of existence will still remain. Others go further. Many modern evangelicals have proposed that hell becomes complete non-existence, that the damned in hell are completely destroyed, without existence or sensation of any kind. Previously scorned as the heresy of Jehovah's witnesses and Seventh Day Adventists, annihilation is quickly becoming an evangelical alternative to believing in endless punishment.

Jewish teachers in Christ's day were divided over whether sinners were purified in Gehenna before being released, tormented forever, or utterly destroyed. Some sources suggested all three might occur. According to the online Jewish Encyclopedia: " *A similar view is expressed in the Babylonian Talmud, which adds that those who have sinned themselves but have not led others into sin remain for twelve months in Gehenna; "after twelve months their bodies are destroyed, their souls are burned, and the wind strews the ashes under the feet of the pious. But as regards the heretics, etc., and Jeroboam, Nebat's son, hell shall pass away, but they shall not pass away" (R. H. 17a; comp. Shab. 33b). All that descend into Gehenna shall come up again, with the exception of three classes of men: those who have committed adultery, or shamed their neighbors, or vilified them (B. M. 58b)."*

Early Christians, however, tended to hold either "eternal punishment" or "purgatorial" views; either way, the human soul exists forever. Yet the arguments made for annihilation deserve recognition as well. Clark Pinnock, one of today's leading theologians to argue for the annihilist view, has the following to say: *"I will maintain that the ultimate result of rejecting God is self-destruction, closure with God, and absolute death in body, soul, and spirit. I take the verse seriously that says "the wages of sin is death.".*

Indeed, whether we find the annihilist argument convincing or not, we must agree that much of the Bible's teaching on damnation uses the language of death and destruction. Death, not eternal punishment, is what the book of Genesis promises to Adam if he disobeys God. In fact, the Old Testament consistently points to destruction and death as the fate of the wicked. Other than one reference in the book of Daniel, eternal punishment is not overtly taught in the Old Testament. The New Testament borrows a phrase from Isaiah to describe hell: *"And they will go out and look upon the dead bodies of those who rebelled against me; their worm will not die, nor will their fire be quenched, and they will be loathsome to all mankind."*[64]

An annihilist would argue that, just as Isaiah's reference describes death rather than conscious existence in a place of punishment, so too do the New Testament references. Pinnock suggests that the Greek belief in the immortality of the soul, which was influential on early Christian thought, has led to the doctrine of eternal hell. Even in the New Testament, Pinnock argues, many of Jesus' fiery warnings result in the wicked being "burned up" rather than "burned forever". Pinnock further argues that the apostle Paul also makes annihilist statements: *"he warned that the wicked would see corruption (Gal 6:8) and stated that God would destroy the wicked (1 Cor 3:17, Phil 1:28) and spoke of their fate as a death that they deserved to die (Romans 1:28)"* It is also worth noting that when the Pharisees and Sadducees ask Jesus to mediate a dispute about the afterlife, Jesus talks about "the worthy" being raised, implying that the others simply remain dead. William Barclay (not himself an annihilist) suggests that Jesus' statement about God *"destroying body and soul in Gehenna"*[65] could be considered evidence for that belief as well. Not all annihilists agree in their understanding of how annihilation occurs. Some believe that only the saved will ever rise from the dead, while the unsaved cease their existence at death (conditional immortality). In this view the soul is naturally mortal, as much of the Old Testament seems to teach, and the saved are given the special gift of immortality by Christ. Other annihilists do believe in hell as a place of punishment. To them, annihilation is a merciful end, a final extinction after sufficient punishment has been meted out to meet the standards of justice. This view attempts to reconcile the scriptural passages on destruction with the passages on punishment after death, such as the story of Lazarus and Dives. In either case, the annihilist cannot believe that eternal punishment can ever be considered just. Rather, the sinner who refuses to enjoy the presence of God is given his wish: non-existence. Clark Pinnock argues as follows: *"the soul is not an immortal substance that has to be placed somewhere if it rejects God. If a person does reject God finally, there is nothing in biblical anthropology to contradict what Jesus plainly taught - God will destroy the wicked, body and soul, in hell."*

    The doctrine of annihilation is an admirable attempt to maintain the need for salvation in Christian theology without defending an eternally - torturing God. It is likely to become more popular, as it lacks the brutality of the literal view of hell, while avoiding some of the large-scale theological revisions that other views on hell require us to make. Prominent Christian leaders such as John Stott, John Wenham and F.F. Bruce have expressed openness to, or even support of the idea.

    The difficulties that I have with the annihilist view (difficulties shared by conservative believers) are threefold. Firstly, while inclusivism and even universalism have a long and storied history in Christian thought, annihilation has rarely been a significant belief until recent times. Secondly, I find some of the Scriptural passages referring to hell are difficult to understand from an annihilation perspective. Max Lucado suggests that *"there is no point on which I'd more gladly be wrong than the eternal duration of hell. If God, on the last day, extinguishes the wicked, I'll celebrate my misreading of his words. Yet annihilation seems inconsistent with Scripture. God sobers his warnings with eternal language."*

    Finally, while eternal non-existence is likely preferable to Jonathan Edward's vision of what hell is like, it is less certain that annihilation is a "kinder" option than a hell described by, say, C.S. Lewis. Many unbelievers in this life choose misery over what they believe to be the non-existence of death; could not the afterlife function the same way? There is a special horror in being extinguished forever, to completely cease to exist.

Theologians Moreland and Habermas argue that *"For the sake of argument, if we compare extinction with life in hell, it is clearly more immoral to extinguish humans with intrinsic value than to allow them to continue living in a state with a low quality of life. In fact, we do not believe the second alternative is immoral at all, but the first alternative is immoral"*... and furthermore *"annihilationism versus the traditionalists regarding hell form a precise parallel to quality-of-life versus sanctity-of-life positions regarding infanticide and euthanasia. Remember, hell is not a torture chamber, and people in hell are not howling like dogs in mind-numbing pain. There are degrees of anguish in hell. But the endlessness of existence in hell at least dignifies the people there by continuing to respect their autonomy and their intrinsic value as persons"*.

In addition to total despair and total annihilation, there is a third possibility. This is the idea that human beings in hell maintain at least some semblance of humanity, at least for some amount of time, as the "rich man" in the book of Luke does. If people retain their mental faculties in hell, and if they are free to interact with each other, will they do so in any meaningful way? It is generally assumed by theologians that, if there is any interaction between persons in hell, it is violent, cruel, and selfish. Mary K. Baxter's "Divine Revelation of Hell", for example, describes damned spirits torturing each other for fun. In Hrovat's "Letter from Beyond" a woman in hell describes her plight at follows: *"All of these memories only show us the horrible sight of the graces we rejected. How this tortures us now! We do not eat, we do not sleep, we do not walk with human legs as you know. Enchained in spirit, we reprobates stare with terror at our misspent lives, howling and gnashing our teeth, tormented and filled with hatred. Do you hear me? Here we drink hatred as if it were water. We all hate one another. And more than anything else, we hate God."*

Serious theologians rarely seem to waste much thought on the interactions that people might have with one another in hell, but there is nothing to prevent me from doing so. If hell is a place where no moral laws are enforced, would the most evil, or most powerful, of all rule like violent prison gangs, unhindered by any guards or outside influences? Or, conversely, if the most sinful of people suffer the most in hell, would that enable the "least bad" to take over? One could almost imagine a group of men and women, who were fairly reasonable persons on earth but nonetheless rejected God, attempting to form their own society even in hell. Such an idea might make a great science fiction story; or would the depths of moral depravity of those in hell make any kind of co-operation impossible?

Lewis' "The Great Divorce" features the damned as ghosts who are perfectly able to interact with others in hell; some of them hold meetings and even run theological societies! However, the ghosts soon spread apart, unable to live together in harmony, spreading further and further into the distance because of their unceasing conflict with each other. In this story, the ghosts have the opportunity to take a bus ride (one marked with much bickering and even violence) to heaven! Through fiction Lewis explores the necessity of hell (the famous "Door Locked from the Inside" theory makes an appearance); the self-centeredness that is characteristic of the damned; and the tantalizing suggestion that if the door to hell is self-locked, there might be a way out.

Much of the novel concerns the saved trying to convert the damned. One by one, the ghosts prove too proud to repent and enter heaven. One refuses to ask for forgiveness because he will not admit error; another will not remain in a heaven that has accepted his law-breaking subordinate, a third persists in wallowing in self-pity; and a woman refuses to enter without regaining control of her (already saved) son. One ghost, however, harassed by a lustful demon on his shoulder, allows the angelic beings to kill the demon and free him. He is instantly and gloriously transformed from a damned ghost to a glorious, heavenly being.

Is such a post-mortem salvation really possible? Lewis himself appeared to be unsure, or at least willing to state with certainty one way or the other. (*"To him, hell will have been purgatory"* he describes those who change their mind in his story.) However, his use of George Macdonald as a hero in the story is revealing. In his own real-life writings, the Scottish author MacDonald argued that hell need not be permanent. He saw hell not as a final end for souls, but as yet another (admittedly severe) attempt by God to draw the sinner to himself. Hell itself, in Macdonald's view, becomes purgatorial, a place of suffering but also of cleaning with the hope of renewal. In Macdonald's own words:

"I believe that justice and mercy are simply one and the same thing. [I believe] such is the mercy of God that he will hold his children in the consuming fire of his distance until they pay the uttermost farthing, until they drop the purse of selfishness with all the dross that is in it, and rush home to the Father and the Son, and the many brethren, rush inside the center of the life-giving fire whose outer circles burn".

MacDonald's thoughts are not the teaching of the mainstream Christian church. However, they are far from his alone. The doctrine of salvation on the other side of death, perhaps even the salvation of most, or all of mankind, is an idea as old as the Christian faith.

Tales from Beyond

Chapter 9

Author: Charles McKaig as quoted by Maurice Rawlings
Setting: Describing his heart attack and subsequent near-death experience.

When I came to, Dr. Rawlings was giving me CPR, and he asked me what was the matter, because I was looking so scared. I told him that I had been to hell and I need help! He said to me, "Keep your hell to yourself, I'm a doctor and I'm trying to save your life, you need a minister for that." As he was giving me CPR, he was trying to install a pacemaker with the other hand. And I would fade out every so often, so then he would focus CPR again and bring me back.

I was soon floating in the air, watching what was going on, looking down. Whenever I would come back to my body, I kept asking, "Please help me, please help me, I don't want to go back to hell." Soon a nurse named Pam said, "He needs help, do something!" At that time, Dr. Rawlings told me to repeat this short prayer. "I believe Jesus Christ is the Son of God. Jesus, save my soul. Keep me alive. If I die, please keep me out of hell!" After that, the other fading out experiences were very pleasant. I saw my stepmother, my mother. My mom passed away when I was about 5 months old. I never saw a photograph of her.

My stepmother passed away about 10 years ago. I did not have any contact with them. All I could remember was that they kept their hands reached out to me.

I've heard it said that you couldn't carry money with you, and when I was with my mother and stepmother, I saw they had no pockets. I know that sounds weird but I was trying to remember everything I saw.

After that, I remember walking down a lane that had colors on both sides, brilliant colors. I had a little experience in Art, but nobody, not ever Rembrandt could reproduce those colors, they were so bright. There was this light that surrounded me; I believe it was the Holy Spirit. It surrounded me and took care of me. I've never felt so good and so safe in my whole life.

Tales from Beyond

Since hell is hopefully something that we will never have to experience ourselves (and if we did we could not return to talk about it) our understanding of hell does not come from first-hand experience. It should be noted, however, that some - very few - persons claim to have experiential knowledge of hell. John the Revelator is not the only one to claim divine revelations of hell; in addition, some who have had a near-death experience talk about a hellish afterlife. Let us examine a few examples. A word of caution; I am in no way qualified to determine the difference between a legitimate God-given vision, a hallucination, and a blatant lie (though I have my own opinions).

I do not believe that a proper understanding of hell is best obtained from so-called "first-hand accounts." However, it is interesting, and possibly useful, to consider a few such accounts and compare them to what we can learn from Scripture and tradition. This chapter might be of interest to some while others should feel free to skip over it. It will be clear that people who claim to experience hell do not all describe it in the same way. Let us begin with a vision of a literal, flaming hell. John Bunyan, author of the Pilgrim's Progress, records that he was about to kill himself when he was interrupted by an angel. The angel not only saved Bunyan's life but also took him on a tour of heaven and hell. In hell (a lake of burning fire) Bunyan encountered several damned souls, who explained to him the nature of their eternal punishment.

"First, we undergo a variety of torment. We are tormented here a thousand, even ten thousand different ways. Those who are the most afflicted on Earth seldom have more than one affliction at a time. If they have the plague, the gout, the stone, and a fever at one time, how miserable they would think of

themselves? Yet all those are but the biting of a flea compared to these intolerable, pungent pains that we endure. Here we have all the loathing variety of hell to grapple with. There is an unquenchable fire here to burn us with: a lake of burning brimstone always choking us; eternal chains to tie us with; utter darkness to frighten us, and our conscience which gnaws on us everlastingly. And any one of these is worse to bear than all the torments mankind has ever felt on Earth".

As in many medieval writings, Bunyan recorded that the damned suffered ironic punishments symbolic of their sins on earth. For example, an excessively greedy woman was tormented by having liquid gold poured down her throat. The woman could only argue that *"If it was gold I would never complain. But he mocks me, and instead of gold he only gives me this horrid, stinking sulfur. If I had my gold I would be happy still, for I value it so much that if I had it, I would not part with it even if an entrance to heaven could be bought."*

Christians today continue to claim divine revelation of the afterlife. Most of the Christian bookstores I have visited are remarkably light on serious theological works studying the doctrine of hell. However, they always seem to carry several books by people who claim to have been there. One of the favorites seems to be Mary K. Baxter's book "a Divine Revelation of Hell". Baxter claims that Jesus herself gave her a length tour of both heaven and hell.

Mary Baxter's hell is a disturbing place. It contains not only the traditional elements of a medieval hell: fire, prison cells, demons, torment; but it seems to be filled mostly with backslidden Christians, screaming to Jesus for mercy as he walks by. Jesus guides her through the various limbs of hell. "Jesus" explains: *"Hell is shaped like a human body lying in the center of the earth. The body is lying on her back, with both arms and both legs stretched out. As I have a body of believers, so hell has a body of sin and death. As the Christ-body is built up daily, so the hell-body is also built up daily."*

In addition to the torment of fire, some people suffer stranger tortures. "All of a sudden, right before my eyes, the woman began to change forms - first to an old, old woman, then to a young woman; to a middle-aged woman and then back to the old lady I had first seen. In shock, I watched as she went through these changes one after the other.... When she saw Jesus, she cried, "Lord, have mercy on me. Let me out of this place of torment."...Again she screamed, "O Lord, let me out of here before they return." She now stood at the front of the cell, clenching the bars with tight fists. She said, "I know Your love is real. I know Your love is true. Let me out!" Then as the woman cried in terror, I saw that something was beginning to rip the flesh from her body....The woman sat back in the chair and began to rock. But now only a skeleton was sitting in the rocking chair - a skeleton with a dirty mist inside. Where there had been a clothed body only minutes ago, now there were blackened and burned bones and empty sockets for eyes. The soul of the woman moaned and cried out to Jesus in repentance. But her cries were too late."

Oddest of all is the "fun center"; a location where demons and souls who were deceived get to torture their deceivers. "In one such torment, spiritual bones were taken apart and buried in different parts of hell. The soul was literally torn apart and the parts scattered across hell in a kind of demonic scavenger hunt. The mutilated souls felt tremendous pain. Those outside the arena could throw stones at those who were in the ring. Every imaginable method of torture was allowed. The souls being tormented cried out for death, but that is eternal death."

The grotesque passages of Mary Baxter's books are, thankfully, not the only supposedly firsthand account of the afterlife. Others teach of a hell more in line with the "metaphorical" view of Billy Graham, Pope John Paul II and C.S. Lewis. In The Great Divorce, Lewis clearly states that he is not "another Swedenborg", attempting to describe the details of the afterlife in factual terms. Nonetheless, Lewis' vision of hell shares distinct similarities with that of Emmanuel Swedenborg, a Swedish mystic who lived in the late 1600's and claimed to have made many visits to heaven and hell. Swedenborg was not the most orthodox of Christians and held some beliefs that might be considered heretical, but his views on hell are interesting nonetheless. Like Lewis, he views hell as a location defined by a person's loathsome choices and selfish evil, rather than as a place where God inflicts external punishment.

Swedenborg's hell is a kind of prison, made up of three kingdoms with various areas corresponding to various moral crimes a person has committed. Swedenborg insists that hell is a self-chosen location. Those who desire evil, rather than good, cannot and will not be happy in heaven and willfully choose to exist in hell instead. He suggests that *"people who are absorbed in evil are connected to hell and actually are there in spirit; and after death they crave above all to be where their evil is. So after death, it is we, not the Lord, who cast ourselves into hell."* Swedenborg explains that *"hell is differentiated into communities... the communities in hell are differentiated according to their evils"*. The inmates run the prison in Swedenborg's hell; the stronger enforce law on the weaker. *"The reason tortures are permitted by the Lord in the hells is that there is no other way evils can be restrained and tamed. Fear of punishment is the only means of controlling and taming evils and keeping the hellish mob in restraints."*

Occasionally, hell does flare into full-on rioting, and angels are called in to restore order through force. In Swedenborg's hell, punishment (other than occasional interference by angels to keep the peace) is inflicted by the denizens of hell on each other. God, the source of only good, does not cause further suffering.

Swedenborg explicitly states that the fire of hell is a metaphor for eternal suffering and unrestrained evil, rather than a literal description of burning. *"Because hellfire is love for oneself and the world, it is also all the craving of those loves, since craving is love reaching out. Whatever we love we constantly crave, and it is our delight, since we feel delight when we get what we love or crave. There is no other source of our heart's delight. So hellfire is the craving and pleasure that well up from these two loves as its sources. These evils are contempt for others, enmity and hostility toward people who do not support us, envy, hatred, and vengefulness; and savagery and cruelty as a result... It does need to be known, though, that the people in the hells are not actually in fire."*

Rather than tormenting those in hell or even neglecting them, Swedenborg's God continues to watch over his fallen creatures from afar, never completely abandoning those who despise him. In addition to maintaining order over his penal facility, God offers small mercies to those in hell. For example, the spirits in hell are woefully deformed by their evil:" *Some of their faces are black, some like little torches, some pimply, with huge ulcerated sores. In many cases there is no visible face, only something hairy or bony in its place.*" However, the Lord in His mercy allows the denizens of hell to see each other as regular people, perhaps to alleviate some of the horror of their self-chosen location.

Among inclusivist or universalist Christians, many are encouraged by the experience of the Catholic mystic Julian of Norwich. Upon asking God about the fate of those who are not Christians, she received the famous answer that *"all shall be well, and all shall be well, and all manner of thing shall be well"*. While Julian's church taught eternal hell, she claimed a different vision.

"*It appears to me that there is a deed that the Holy Trinity shall do on the last day, and when that deed shall be done and how it shall be done is unknown to all creatures under Christ, and shall be until it has been done. - This is the great deed ordained by our Lord God from eternity, treasured up and hidden in his blessed breast, only known to himself, and by this deed he shall make all things well; for just as the Holy Trinity made all things from nothing, so the Holy Trinity shall make all well that is not well.*

"*And I wondered greatly at this revelation, and considered our faith, wondering as follows; our faith is grounded in God's word, and it is part of our faith that we should believe that God's word will be kept in all things; and one point of our faith is that many shall be damned. And given all this, I thought it impossible that all manner of things should be well, as our Lord revealed at this time. And I received no other answer in showing from our Lord God but this. "What is impossible to you is not impossible to me. I shall keep my word in all things and I shall make all things well."*

In addition people who claim to have seen visions of hell, there are those who have actually experienced clinical death. Near-death experiences (NDE's) are fascinating for people of all faiths and backgrounds. Could the near-death experiences of people help teach us about the realities of the afterlife?

First a note of caution: neither Christians nor Non-Christians are unanimous in their belief that the near-death experience is an actual visit to the afterlife. Non-believing scientists and some believers too, consider it a natural phenomenon caused by loss of oxygen to a dying brain, rather than a truly supernatural experience. Christians are perplexed because some, but not all, near-death experiences fall in line with Christian eschatology. In fact, Christians often meet Jesus in their near-death experiences, while those of other faiths might meet different religious leaders. Neither Christians nor secular scientists are sure why near-death experiences are recounted by some but not all people who experience clinical death and are brought back to live. Dr. Maurice Rawlings suggests that people who are interviewed right after being resuscitated are more likely to remember their NDE. Regardless of one's opinion on the subject, however, NDE's are interesting and offer what might - just might - be first hand experiences of heaven and hell.

Near- death experiences have been recorded by many people who underwent clinical death (heart arrest) and were then resuscitated. Dr. Raymond Moody, the first person to study near-death experiences clinically, argued that the following steps take place during the "typical" NDE: A strange sound which Moody describes as "buzzing"; a feeling of peace and painlessness; an out of body experience that has been liked to floating away from one's body; the experience of travelling through a tunnel (towards the light at the end) or, alternatively, rising towards the heavens; meeting people of light, often relatives or other loved ones who have already died; a powerful Being of Light (sometimes, but not always identified as Jesus); a "Life Review" (life flashing before your eyes) and a reluctant return to life.

It should be noted that, according to near-death researchers, the vast majority of near-death experiences are heavenly in nature. This includes both Christian and non-Christian experiences. One is tempted to conclude that the near-death experience, if it is accepted as a legitimate experience of the afterlife, is a powerful argument in favor of inclusive salvation. If NDE's are legitimate journeys into the afterlife then it seems that "the many" rather than "the few" attain salvation.

Nonetheless, hellish near-death experiences do exist. Dr. Maurice Rawlins converted from atheism to Christianity after reviving a man whose heart stopped several times. When Rawlins applied CPR, the man began to scream that he was in hell and begged Rawlins to save his life so that he would not go back. In "beyond Death's Door" and "To Hell and Back" Rawlins recounts these and other stories about NDE's, many of them hellish ones.

Rawlins himself was at a loss to explain why. Although his theology taught him that only a few would be saved, positive near-death experiences were more common than hellish ones. Rawlins made several suggestions:

1. The Non-Christian who sees a heavenly afterlife is deceived. The devil, masquerading as an "angel of light", prevents the person from seeing how close they are to hell and thus their need for a savior.

2. Hellish near-death experiences are so disturbing that people quickly repress them, or otherwise refuse to share them. This suggests that hellish NDE's might be more common than are reported.

3. Some people have both a hellish and then a heavenly experience; that is, they fall into hell, cry out for mercy to Jesus, and are immediately rescued. Such an experience might be foreign to evangelical theology, but many Catholics would recognize the teaching that persons can quite literally choose their allegiance to God - or not - at the moment of death. According to Rawlins, this was a common occurrence; many hellish NDE's turn into heavenly ones, following some sort of conversion.

In the Journal of Near-Death Studies, Atwater makes the following observations on hellish NDE's:

"Of the hell-like cases 1 have found, I have yet to come across an individual who reported a fiery hot or burning sensation during the experience itself, although I have spoken with researchers who have. If a sensation of temperature was felt, the majority in the study I conducted commented on how cold it was, or clammy, or shivery, or "icy hard." Also mentioned was the dullness of the light, even grayness, as if overcast, foggy, or somehow "heavy." Many experienced a bright light beckoning to them initially, but

when they entered the light it promptly dimmed or darkened."

Dr. Howard Stern describes his hellish near-death experience, in which he is tormented not by temperature but by others:

"Hours ago, I had hoped to die and end the torment of life. Now things were worse as I was forced by a mob of unfriendly and cruel people toward some unknown destination in the darkness. They began shouting and hurling insults at me, demanding that I hurry along. And they refused to answer any question.

Finally, I told them that I wouldn't go any farther. At that time they changed completely. They became much more aggressive and insisted that I was going with them. A number of them began to push and shove me, and I responded by hitting back at them. A wild orgy of frenzied taunting, screaming and hitting ensued. I fought like a wild man. All the while it was obvious that they were having great fun."

Increasingly desperate as the attack continued, Storm reverted to the religious phrases he had learned in his youth.

"Exactly what happened was ... and I'm not going to try and explain this. From inside of me I felt a voice, my voice, say, "Pray to God." My mind responded to that, "I don't pray. I don't know how to pray." This is a guy lying on the ground in the darkness surrounded by what appeared to be dozens if not hundreds and hundreds of vicious creatures who had just torn him up. The situation seemed utterly hopeless, and I seemed beyond any possible help whether I believed in God or not. The voice again told me to pray to God. It was a dilemma since I didn't know how. The voice told me a third time to pray to God. I started saying things like, "The Lord is my shepherd, I shall not want ... God bless America" and anything else that seemed to have a religious connotation."

The attackers left him alone when he began to call out to God. When Howard called to Jesus specifically, he encountered Jesus as a "Being of Light" from a typical NDE.

"I knew that this radiant being was powerful. It was making me feel so good all over. I could feel its light on me – like very gentle hands around me. And I could feel it holding me. But it was loving me with overwhelming power. After what I had been

through, to be completely known, accepted, and intensely loved by this Being of Light surpassed anything I had known or could have imagined. I began to cry and the tears kept coming and coming. And we, I and this light, went up and out of there."

Howard, for one, believes that people after death can still be rescued from hell. Near-death expert Dr. Vincent, who himself suffered a hellish experience, suggests that *"Almost no one who has ever studied the near-death experience (NDE) comes away thinking that Hell is eternal."*

The near-death experience in itself is not enough to give us a detailed theology of the afterlife. In fact, some people's NDE's are difficult to reconcile with Christian theology. Those who do not believe in hell must face the fact the hellish NDE's occur, while those who do (especially Christian exclusivists) may be baffled by their relative rarity. Nonetheless, they remind us that the afterlife is not merely an intellectual exercise, but rather an experience we must all go through. To some people, heaven and hell are already as real as everyday life, and many of them believe that those is hell can still cry out to God.

Escape from Hell

Chapter 10

Author: Brain McLaren in "The Last Word and the Word After That "
Setting: A young woman speaking to her father, a pastor, about her Bible Study
Narrator: Jess Poole

"She tells me that before God ever created the universe, he decided to create some people who would be blessed forever and others who would be damned forever. Then I say that sounds cruel, and she tells me it had to be that way, because the blessed would never have any idea of how blessed they are unless they had something to compare it to. I said that sounded crazy and sick, and she told me to look up the words election and predestination in the Bible and I'd be convinced.
Then Daddy, maybe I shouldn't have said this, but I said if that's what the Bible teaches, then I don't believe the Bible anymore, and if God is going to send all my friends to hell, then he can send me right along with them because I love them, and I'd rather be loyal to them than save my own skin, but I didn't exactly say skin, if you know what I mean daddy, which shocked her and really got her mad. I said I could never be happy in a party upstairs in the heavenly living room knowing that so many people were being tortured in the basement, and I thought it was pretty heartless of her to think she could be happy under those circumstances. In fact, I told her that I thought God would be disgusted to have people like that at his party and that I thought God himself would go down into the basement to help the people there.
So she says that I feel that way because I'm looking from a

human point of view, and I don't understand God's holiness and justice, and God's ways are higher than ours and whatever, and I was like totally appalled at this, and I told her that didn't sound holy and just, it sounded sadistic, and my Dad didn't teach me a sadistic version of Christianity. So she said that you weren't teaching the truth anyway, which is what Clarissa Zeamer told her, and now she knew Clarissa was right.
At that point [boyfriend] Caid speaks up and says, real serious, "Hey Joanna, I've got a question for you. You seem very knowledgeable about hell and all, and I've always wondered: Who's more likely to go to hell- homosexuals or those dudes who carry the "God hates fags" signs? I mean, is it more serious to fool around with the wrong gender or to portray God as an ignorant, hateful bigot?"

Escape from Hell

In his autobiography, the famed Bible scholar William Barclay unabashedly supports a universalist theology. He believes that hell exists, but that it does not have the last word in the human story.

"In one thing I would go beyond strict orthodoxy - I am a convinced universalist. I believe in the end all will be gathered into the love of God. Gregory of Nyssa... believed in [universalism] because of the character of God. *"Being good, God entertains pity for fallen man; being wise, he is not ignorant of the means for his recovery." Second, he believed in it because of* the nature of evil. *Evil must in the end be moved out of existence.... Third, he believed in it because of* the purpose of punishment. *The purpose of punishment is always remedial. Jesus said, 'When I am lifted up from the earth I will draw all to myself' (John 12:32). Paul writes: 'God has consigned all to disobedience that he may have mercy on all' (Romans 11:32). 'As in Adam all die, so in Christ shall all be made alive' (1 Corinthians 15:28). The New Testament itself is not in the least afraid of the word* all.
Matthew 25:46 says the rejected go away to eternal punishment and the righteous to eternal life. The Greek word for punishment

is kolasis... [which] originally meant the pruning of trees to make them grow better. It is never used for anything but remedial punishment. The word for eternal is aionios, which cannot be used properly by anyone but God. Eternal punishment is then literally that kind of remedial punishment which it befits God to give and which only God can give...

I believe it is impossible to set limits to the grace of God... I believe that the grace of God is as wide as the universe. [And] I believe in the ultimate and complete triumph of God, when all things will be subject to him, and when God will be everything to everyone.

God is not only King and Judge, God is Father. *No father could be happy while there were members of his family forever in agony. The only victory love can enjoy is the day when its offer of love is answered by the return of love. The only possible final triumph is a universe loved by and in love with God."*

Barclay neatly and correctly highlights the arguments to be made for what many view as a heresy. First of all, he points out that Christians throughout church history have made coherent arguments for universal salvation. Whatever else universalism may be, it is not simply the product of "modern sentimentality" as some conservative Christians allege. Early church fathers such as Gregory of Nyssa and Origen clearly believed that, in the end, all people will be saved. Origen, the man most associated with universalism, taught systematically on the subject, believing Scripture defended his belief. *"Stronger than all the evils in the soul is the Word, and the healing power that dwells in Him, and this healing He applies, according to the will of God, to everyman. The consummation of all things is the destruction of evil...to quote Zephaniah: "My determination to gather the nations, that I may assemble kingdoms, to pour upon them my indignation, even all my fierce anger, for all the earth shall be devoured with the fire of my jealousy. For then will I turn to the people a pure language that they may all call upon the name of the Lord, to serve Him with one consent"...Consider carefully the promise, that all shall call upon the Name of the Lord, and serve him with one consent."*

If universalism is a heresy, it is one as old as the Christian faith. The kind of universalism Barclay and Origen followed, the type of universalism I want to explore, does not deny the existence of hell. In Christian universalism, hell is quite real and quite awful ("All the earth shall be devoured with fire" is hardly a pleasant thought). What Christian Universalists dispute is not the existence of hell, but rather its purpose and duration. The universalist hell serves the same function as purgatory, a temporary place of preparation for sinners, in the hope that one day they might be fit for heaven. The Church Father Diodore of Tarsus explained: *"For the wicked there are punishments, not perpetual, however, lest the immortality prepared for them should be a disadvantage, but they are to be purified for a brief period according to the amount of malice in their works. They shall therefore suffer punishment for a short space, but immortal blessedness having no end awaits them...the penalties to be inflicted for their many and grave sins are very far surpassed by the magnitude of the mercy to be showed to them."*

Barclay points out that the Bible itself can be used to support universal salvation. The universalist needs not reject the words of scripture. Jesus himself, and especially the apostle Paul, make arguments that are most easily understood from a universalist perspective. The Bible's "proof-texts" for eternal punishment, on the other hand, are not immune to reinterpretation. Scripture is not as unequivocally on the side of the traditional view as many Christians believe.

Finally, if such a thing is even necessary, Barclay points out the benefits of a universalist theology. He who believes in universal reconciliation believes that God is always good, always wishes the good of mankind and uses His power to bring all people to salvation. If God is Love, if God *"is willing that no man should perish, but that all should come to repentance"*, then universalism makes good sense. It is much easier to believe that God is good when you know that God is good to everyone at all times, and that God does not give up on people.

Believing in temporary, rather than eternal hell solves many of the problems discussed in these chapters. The exact nature of suffering in hell becomes less important if we take that suffering to be remedial, meted out for the benefit of the sufferer rather than at the pleasure of God. Fire, darkness, beatings, isolation, or whatever descriptor we may choose; we can be assured that the severity of suffering will be exactly what is needed, neither excessive nor ineffective. The common argument against God's justice, that finite sins should not warrant infinite punishment, is moot of hell is not eternal. And the debates between predestinarians and Arminians, between inclusivists and exclusivists, become less important if human death is not the final opportunity to be saved. If everyone (or almost everyone) will one day be saved, the details about who gets in immediately are less pressing.

Most conservative Christians have rejected Barclay, George Macdonald and Origen's worldview. Many Christian conservatives see universalism as the most dreadful of heresies. The evangelical church, especially, continues to oppose universalist theology with a passion. Mainline protestant denominations are generally much more accepting, or at least tolerant, of the idea. A quick search on the internet bears witness to this virulence that accompanies many hell debates. A rather gruesome example is found on the theology forum www.theologyonline.com in which a traditional poster berates a Christian universalist: *"I know you don't preach The Gospel, so you are already accursed. I pray you'll repent, but I am not going to hold my breath... No, you don't understand The Word of God or represent Him in this earth. You represent a 'kinder gentler god' that doesn't even exist. The Judge of the Universe does exist, and He is not mocked. He will recompense evil. He is God, not universalistic nightmares of a limp-wristed god that doesn't do anything about evil."*

Unlike William Barclay, I am not a convinced universalist myself. If I were, I would not struggle over the doctrine of hell as I do. And so I will offer the objections against universalism as best a can, present the universalist response and leave it for the reader to decide if universalism is a viable, or true, understanding of Christian salvation.

Objection # 1. Universalism has been rejected by most Christians.
In their book "If Grace is True", universalists Gulley and Mulholland suggest that in the first few hundred years of Christianity, universalism was a popular or even a majority belief. This belief in universal salvation was exemplified by the

teachings of Clement of Alexandria and Origen. Edward Beecher suggests that four pre-eminent theological schools in early Christendom were universalist, while one taught annihilation and the other eternal punishment. St. Augustine (354-430 AD) admitted that *"many, while not denying the scriptures, believe there will be an end to the punishments of the damned"* although he himself was a strong proponent of eternal punishment. The official church began to follow Augustine's teaching and universalism was officially condemned as a heresy as 553 AD. It has never recovered as an orthodox belief, though universalists have always been a minority group among Christians. Jonathan Edwards, for example, wrote intensively against the universalists, realizing their belief system was a threat to his. In today's world universalism enjoys a resurgence among Christians.

Objection # 2. Without the threat of hell, people will sin. Hell has always been used as a deterrent. Yet does not a temporary hell also have deterrent value? Do not most of God's warnings in Scripture relate to temporary, rather than everlasting, punishment? The Christian Universalist does not deny the existence of hell, but merely the infinite duration thereof. It is foolish to suggest that a temporal punishment, let alone an age-long punishment, has no value as a deterrent. In fact, several of Jesus' parables reference severe but finite punishment.
William Barclay too, argues that a temporary hell is still a place to be avoided. As all of us know, temporal suffering is still painful. *"It is claimed that [Universalism] takes the iron out of Christianity because it removes the threat. No longer can the sinner be dangled over the pit of hell. No longer can what Burns called the "hangmen's whip" of the fear of hell be threateningly cracked over the sinner. But the kind of universalism in which I believe has not simply obliterated hell and said that everything will be all right for everyone; it has stated grimly that, if you will have it so, you can go to Heaven via Hell."* The website tentmaker.org phrases it more colloquially but no less effectively: "*All that universalism per se rules out here is the "infinitely big stick". As I've stressed, universalism itself does not rule out that there will be punishment for some after death. Indeed, it does not rule out that there will be a lot of punishment for some. So it's not only consistent with the existence of sticks, but with very big -*

indeed, immensely huge- sticks…"

Objection # 3. Universalism over-rides human free will. Clark Pinnock is a vocal critic of the traditional view of hell, and he has written books defending both inclusivism and annihilationism. He draws the line at universalism, however, because he considers it a form of divine coercion that violates the human freedom that God takes so seriously. *"God does not save people against their will, and the existence of hell underlines how seriously he takes the gift of human freedom… to be a universalist one really has to have to work with a predestinarian theology… In such theologies, God is always forcing people to do what they do not want to do. All that would have to happen is for God to increase the number of elect to one hundred percent and save everyone by sovereign (coercive) grace."*

Not surprisingly, Lewis has similar thoughts. *"If the happiness of a creature lies in self-surrender, no one can make that surrender but that person (though others may help), and the person may refuse. I would pay any price to be able to say truthfully 'All will be saved'. But my reason retorts, 'Without their will or with it?' If I say 'without their will' I at once perceive a contradiction; how can the supreme voluntary act of self-surrender be involuntary? If I say 'With their will', my reason replies 'How if they will not give in?"*

This is a worthy critique. Few people will, presumably, enjoy their stay in hell, but will they want to experience the presence of God instead? Or will they stubbornly hold the door shut on themselves, hating God even more than they hate their current situation?

A lot of universalists label themselves "soft" universalists or "hopeful" universalists; that is, they hope and believe that all will eventually be saved, but because of the stubbornness of mankind they concede it may only be "most". Universalists hope and believe that, when confronted with the miseries of hell and the potential glory of heaven, most people will turn from their sin and welcome the opportunity to be purified and eventually saved (in contrast to the "The Great Divorce", where most of the damned refuse salvation on the doorstep of heaven itself).

Objection # 4: Universalism is an anti-Biblical teaching. The fourth objection is probably the most serious. If the Word of

God is to be the final word on the afterlife, let us look at Scripture. Traditionalists are quite correct: there is no verse in the Bible that states "and then the damned will leave hell and be welcomed into heaven" or anything similar. Yet this has not stopped universalist theologians.

The number of Bible verses that feature the word "all" or "the world" in conjunction with salvation is staggering. The traditional (eternal hell believing) theologian needs to interpret these verses selectively, so that "all" does not really mean "all", in order to maintain a consistent theology. The universalist theologian simply inverts the picture; he assumes that when Jesus promises to "draw all people to himself", he means it, and that verses about punishment need to be viewed through the lens of universal salvation. Mercy Aiken and Gary Arimault (among others) on the website tentmaker.org list many

"universalist passages", which suggest a universalist (or at least a strong inclusivist) worldview by the author. A few of my favorites are included here. Most are from the letters of Paul; some are from Jesus Himself.

John 3:17 *"God did not send his son into the world to condemn the world, but in order that <u>the world</u> might be saved through him."*

John 12:32 *"But I, when I am lifted up from the earth, will draw <u>all</u> men to myself."*

Ephesians 1:9,10 *"And he made known to us the mystery of his will according to his good pleasure, which he purposed in Christ, to be put into effect when the times will have reached their fulfillment—to bring <u>all things</u> in heaven and on earth together under one head, even Christ."*

Romans 5:18: *Consequently, just as the result of one trespass was condemnation for all men, so also the result of one act of righteousness was justification that brings life for <u>all</u> men. For just as through the disobedience of the one man the many were made sinners, so also through the obedience of the one man the many will be made righteous.*

Romans 11:32 *For God has bound all men over to disobedience so that he may have mercy on them <u>all</u>.*

Philippians 2:10-11: "*At the name of Jesus <u>every</u> knee should bow, in heaven and on earth and under the earth, and every*

tongue confess that Jesus Christ is Lord, to the glory of God the Father."
1 Timothy 4:10 *"We have our hope set on the living God, who is the Savior of all people, especially of those who believe.*
1 Corinthians 15:21. *"For since death came through a man, the resurrection of the dead comes also through a man. For as in Adam all die, so in Christ all will be made alive."*

    Many of Paul's statements are so straightforward, so shocking, that any other conservative Christian making those statements would surely be accused of heresy. Any theology of hell that wishes to remain truly Biblical must account for these and other Bible verses which seem to suggest that all will eventually be saved.

    Even the Old Testament, which doesn't say much about heaven or hell, declares in circumspect terms that death does not end God's love, even for evildoers. King David rejoiced that "even if I make my bed in Sheol (once translated "hell") you are there."[66] Other Old Testament teachings:

    2 Samuel 14:*14 "For we will surely die and become like water spilled on the ground, which cannot be gathered up again. Yet God does not take away a life; but He devises means, so that His banished ones are not expelled from Him"*

    Lamentations 3:31-33 *"For men are not cast off by the Lord forever. Though he may punish cruelly, yet he will have compassion in the fullness of his love; he does not willingly afflict or punish any mortal man."*

    Universalists also point out that the Biblical city of Sodom, utterly destroyed by an actual fire from heaven, is often used as a symbol for the hellish punishment awaiting sinners in both the Old and the New Testament. Yet the prophet Ezekiel describes the Sodomites as people who will be restored:

    "However, I will restore the fortunes of Sodom and her daughters and of Samaria and her daughters, and your fortunes along with them so that you may bear your disgrace and be ashamed of all you have done in giving them comfort. And your sisters, Sodom with her daughters and Samaria with her daughters, will return to what they were before; and you and your daughters will return to what you were before." [67]

    Finally, consider the bizarre 11th chapter of Romans,

where Paul seems to turn conventional doctrine on its head. It is with good reason that Romans 11 is a puzzling chapter. Paul has been harshly criticizing his own people, the Israelites, for their violent rejection of Jesus over the past few chapters. The Jews have judged themselves "unworthy of eternal life", Paul warns, explaining his choice to evangelize the Gentiles. A group of more determined Christ-rejecters would be difficult to find. The first-century Jews that Paul criticizes saw Jesus face to face, witnesses his miracles, and heard witnesses tell of His resurrection first hand and yet many still refused to repent and believe. Those who believe in predestination often consider Romans 9 (addressing the same Christ-rejecting people) their proof text that God has already chosen to send some people to hell.

"God gave them a spirit of stupor, eyes so that they could not see and ears so that they could not hear, to this very day."[68] Paul does not mince words when describing his countrymen or God's frustration with them. Then Paul shifts his thinking, in ways I am not sure I understand...

"I do not want you to be ignorant of this mystery, brothers, so that you may not be conceited: Israel has experienced a hardening in part until the full number of the Gentiles has come in... As far as the gospel is concerned, they are enemies on your account; but as far as election is concerned, they are loved on account of the patriarchs, for God's gifts and his call are irrevocable. Just as you who were at one time disobedient to God have now received mercy as a result of their disobedience, so they too have now become disobedient in order that they too may now receive mercy as a result of God's mercy to you. For God has bound all men over to disobedience so that he may have mercy on them all."[69]

Unless I radically misunderstand Paul, he considers God to have one final plan: to have mercy on all. Even the hardening of Israel is another opportunity for God to show mercy. This chapter shows a God who will not deviate from his covenant to defeat sin. Those who consider universalism to have no place in Scripture must wrestle with the Apostle Paul's confidence that "the full number of the Gentiles" will come to God, and that all Israel will be saved. Barclay's commentary on this section reads

"God's purpose was a purpose of salvation and not of

destruction. It may well be that Paul would even have gone to the lengths of saying that God's arranging of things was designed to save men and women even against their will. In the last analysis, it was not the wrath of God which was pursuing them, but the love of God which was tracking them down."

Let us turn to the Gospels. Jesus, whose parables often emphasize judgment, also highlight the willingness of God tp save everyone. The Parables of the Lost Coin and the Lost Sheep end in the rescue of all. In the Sermon on the Mount, Jesus contrasts the character of man with that of God. Whereas man is selfish and evil, God is forgiving and generous. *"Be merciful , as your heavenly father is merciful*[72.] Jesus says, mercy is the trademark of God. It is a mercy that extends even to His enemies, a mercy that Jesus prays for as he is nailed to the cross: "Father , forgive then, for they know not what they do."[73]

The Christian universalist must do more than make a Biblical case for universalism. He must be able to discuss the Bible verse that speaks about eternal damnation. The doctrine of eternal punishment (as opposed to temporal punishment after death) hangs largely on the interpretation of the single Greek word *aionios*. In 1875, John Wesley Hanson wrote *"It is not going too far to say that if the Greek Aión - Aiónios does not denote endless duration, then endless punishment is not taught in the Bible"*. In fact, a google search of *aionis* immediately brings up websites defending and attacking universalism. The Greek word, from which we get the English word eon (and the Hebrew *olam,* which is generally considered equivalent in meaning), is a slippery word with multiple possible meanings.

A careful study of Scripture suggests that the Bible uses the word *aionios* for both temporal and eternal events. The meaning appears to be largely determined by context. In addition, Barclay contends that the word *aional* describes something as connected with the eternal God, rather than describing definite or indefinite period of time. In Barclay's view *"aionion"* punishment is punishment from the eternal God.

John Wesley Hanson has this to say*: "applied to Jonah's residence in the fish, [aionios] means seventy hours; to the priesthood of Aaron, it signifies several centuries; to the mountains, thousands of years; to the punishments of a merciful*

God, as long as is necessary to vindicate his law and reform his children; to God himself, eternity. What great is to size, aiónios is to duration. Human beings live from a few hours to a century; nations from a century to thousands of years; and worlds, for aught we know, from a few to many millions of years, and God is eternal. So that when we see the word applied to a human life it denotes somewhere from a few days to a hundred years; when it is applied to a nation, it denotes anywhere from a century to ten thousand years, more or less, and when to God it means endless. In other words it practically denotes indefinite duration."

If the word *aionios* can apply to both temporal and eternal things, which is the proper meaning when referring to God's punishment in hell? Christians have long been disposed to consider *aionian* punishment as unending punishment. St Augustine made a strong case for everlasting hell. He argued, quite reasonably, from the Parable of the Sheep and the Goats:[70] *"they will go to aionian punishment, but the righteous to aionian life."* In Matthew's parable the word *aionios* describes both the "eternal life" of the blessed and "eternal punishment" of the damned. If both are the same length, Augustine reasoned, then hell must last as long as heaven: forever. This argument is still commonly used today, and we should not lightly dismiss what the majority of Christians in history have taught. However, neither should the universalist argument be ignored. I leave it to the reader to decide if Augustine's or Barclay's interpretation of the parable (he argues for remedial punishment) is superior.

In Scripture, it seems to me, two images sit side by side: a vivid depiction of wrath and destruction, and a picture of a God who will do anything to reconcile his children to himself. The New Testament speaks clearly of both; the book of Revelation warns of the "Lake of Fire" for sinners, and in the next chapter it speaks of the River of Life from whom all who wish may drink, while the Spirit and the Bride say "come!". Teilhard de Chadrain expresses the paradox; *"To put the mystery precisely, we must believe two doctrines: (1) the almighty power of God who wants all people to be saved, and (2) the possibility of eternal perdition for those living and dying without love and friendship with God. We must accept these two doctrines without fully understanding how they can be reconciled."*

Christain sotoriology (study of salvation) is filled with paradox. Professor Tom Talbot pragmatically sums up the paradox when he suggests that there are 3 incompatible statements Scripture seems to make in regard to the ultimate destiny of sinful mankind:

1. God wants to save all sinners (2 Peter 3:9: *"The Lord... is not willing that any should perish, but that all should come to repentance"*; 1 Timothy 2:4; God *"desires all men to be saved and to come to the knowledge of the truth";*)

2. God is able to accomplish His wishes (Job 42:2: *"I know that you can do all things; no purpose of yours can be thwarted."* and Colossians 1:19-20 *For God was pleased to have all his fullness dwell in him, and through him to reconcile to himself all things, whether things on earth or things in heaven, by making peace through his blood, shed on the cross*).

3. Some people will never be reconciled to God. (Matt 25: 46 *"They will go into eternal punishment"*, Jude 1:13 *"They are wild waves of the sea, foaming up their shame; wandering stars, for whom blackest darkness has been reserved forever."*)

Professor Talbot points out that Christians have taken different routes to resolving this paradox. Calvinists reject the first premise, and believe that God only wants some people to be saved. Jonathan Edwards, for example, writes unabashedly about God's hatred of the reprobate, and His glorification in their torment. Armenian Christians (those who believe that man's free will, rather than God's predestination, determines who will go to heaven or hell) reject the second of Talbot's statements, and believe that sinful men have the power to thwart God's redemptive purposes.

Universalists, on the other hand, accept the first two premises, and reject the third: eternal hell. Why is it (according to Talbot) that Calvinists and Armenian Christians are often able to tolerate each other, but treat Universalists as dangerous heretics? Is it because the proof for proposition 3 is greater than for the first two? Robert Ingersoll muses: *"Strange! that no one has ever been persecuted by the church for believing God bad, while hundreds of millions have been destroyed for thinking him good. The Orthodox Church will never forgive the universalist for saying, "God is love." It has always been considered one of the very highest evidences of true and undefiled religion that all men, women and children deserve eternal damnation. It has always been heresy to say, "God will at last save all."'*

If the Bible tantalizes readers with the possibility that all will someday be saved, it is short on the details of how that might occur. The book of 1 Peter may provide some details of what William Barclay calls a "breath-taking doctrine of a second chance". In chapter 3 Peter mysteriously announces *"For Christ died for sins once for all, the righteous for the unrighteous, to bring you to God. He was put to death in the body but made alive by the Spirit, through whom also he went and preached to the spirits in prison who disobeyed long ago when God waited patiently in the days of Noah while the ark was being built."*[71]

This rather bizarre section of Scripture seems to suggest that Jesus, upon his death, preached to those who died in Noah's flood (the population of Earth, minus Noah's family.) Unfortunately, the verse does not specify what Jesus said to those "spirits", or what the result was.

In the next chapter, Peter suggests that the judgment of some might occur only after they have a second chance at the gospel: *"they will give account to Him who is ready to judge the living and the dead. For the gospel has for this purpose been preached even to those who are dead, that though they are judged in the flesh as men, they may live in the spirit according to the will of God."* [72]

These are difficult Scriptures, not particularly clear in meaning. The correct understanding of these verses remains highly controversial; many conservative scholars do not accept Barley's interpretation. However, both ancient and modern Christians have considered the possibility that Christ Himself "descended into hell", as the Apostle's creed says, in order to give those imprisoned there a second chance. Was this salvation offered for everyone, or only those without a previous opportunity to repent? Will another, future chance be given? We do not know, but I think we have permission to hope. I once expressed concern to a pastor about the unsaved masses in India, and he told me that my concern was God-given. "God loves the people in India much more than you do, and he is much more concerned for their salvation than you are." This pastor was not a universalist, but even he realized that the goodness of God transcends traditional doctrinal boundaries. We may not understand the details, but we can hope, as the early Christians did, that God's grace reaches everywhere, even beyond the footsteps of missionaries, even beyond the grave.

Whether we find the Biblical arguments for universal salvation convincing or not, we should consider at least that universal salvation emphasizes both the goodness and the triumph of Jesus Christ. If Jesus came to earth to rescue humanity, has he succeeded? John Calvin argued that "Christ is more powerful to save than Adam was to ruin"; he solved the apparent dilemma by insisting that Christ only wanted to save a few. The Apostle Paul seems more optimistic; *"just as the result of one trespass was condemnation for all men, so also the result of one act of righteousness was justification that brings life for all men. For just as through the disobedience of one man the many were made sinners, so also through the obedience of the one man the many will be made righteous."*[73]

Objection # 5: Eternal Hell displays God's glory
Many traditional theologians question the idea that Christ is equally glorified by hell as He is by salvation. Charles Finney wrote that *"saints and angels will be entirely satisfied with the justice of God in the damnation of sinners. They will never take delight in the misery of the damned, but in the display of justice, in the vindication of his insulted majesty and injured honour, in the respect which punishment will create for the law and character of God, they will have pleasure; they will see that the display of his justice is glorious, and will cry halleluiah, while "the smoke of their torment shall ascend up forever and ever."*

Not surprisingly, Jonathan Edwards held a similar view. *"Thus it will be with you that are in an unconverted state, if you continue in it; the infinite might, and majesty, and terribleness of the omnipotent God shall be magnified upon you, in the ineffable strength of your torments. You shall be tormented in the presence of the holy angels, and in the presence of the Lamb; and when you shall be in this state of suffering, the glorious inhabitants of heaven shall go forth and look on the awful spectacle, that they may see what the wrath and fierceness of the Almighty is; and when they have seen it, they will fall down and adore that great power and majesty."*

In this view, the vengeance of God is a glorious thing. I admit I feel drawn towards this view sometimes. It is not hard to believe that I might feel some satisfaction in watching the great monsters of history- the Hitlers and Stalins and Mao Tse Tung's receive their just rewards. If the street gangsters who inspire terror in my beloved Cape Town and the abusive relatives that raped and abused so many of my students will someday face divine justice, will I not applaud? Perhaps I will.

Perhaps all Christians, like the saints beneath the altar in the book of Revelation, should wait in anticipation for God to pour out his vengeance. And yet, I cannot help thinking with William Barclay, that this is a sub-Christian thought. The book of Timothy, Paul tells us that God wants that *"all men would be saved and come to a knowledge of the truth"*.[74] The apostle Peter, himself, the subject of violent persecution, thought that God is *"not willing that any should perish, but that all should come to repentance"*[75]. King David, soaked in the blood of his enemies and under God's judgment himself, praised God with these words: *"The Lord is compassionate and merciful; slow to get angry and filled with unfailing love. He will not constantly accuse us, nor remain angry forever. He does not punish us for all our sins, he does not deal harshly with us as we deserve."*[76]

The Bible tells us that God forgave a murderer and adulterer like David, a coward like Peter, that Jesus healed the ear of a man who arrested him and prayed for the forgiveness of those crucifying him, and that he made his number one enemy called Saul into his greatest apostle and the author of much of the New Testament. (A thought experiment for the reader: Did the soldiers who crucified Jesus receive forgiveness? If so, why? If not, what does that say about Jesus' power to forgive sins?)

From a God this forgiving, how can we not at least consider the possibility of universal salvation? If all those who repent in this life, no matter how awful they may be, receive a divine pardon, will God then shut the door of heaven in their face after death?

It seems to me that, while the Scriptures (the Old Testament especially) overflow with the wrath and judgment of

God, the purpose generally serves a positive point; to turn the sinful back to God. The prophets speak often of God being torn, conflicted, and moved by the wrath He feels necessary to pour down in mankind. It seems to me that God hardly delights in his punishment (*"I take no pleasure from the death of the wicked"*.[77]) Rather, He rejoices when the day of wrath is over and reconciliation can begin.

One example among many: Isaiah 8 describes the punishment of the sinful: *"Distressed and hungry, they will roam through the land. When they are famished; they will become enraged and, looking upward, will curse their king and their God. Then they will look toward the earth and see only distress and darkness and fearful gloom, and they will be thrust into utter darkness."*[78] Isaiah 9 trumpets proudly the temporary nature of that condemned state, and the Savior that God will one day raise up: *"Nevertheless, there will be no more gloom for those who were in distress... The people walking in darkness have seen a great light; on those living in the land of the shadow of death a light has dawned."*[79] The Biblical God is willing to condemn, but he is glorified when He saves. Even if hell is eternal, I believe that to be a source of divine sorrow, not joy. *"God hates hell and he hates people going there"*, according to conservative scholar J.P. Moreland.

I have seen God's saving grace in the likes of Cape Town criminals. I have shaken hands with converted prisoners, who have risked their lives to leave their gangs and follow Christ. I have spoken with a warden who told me that the presence of Christ was visible in his cell block and that violence had decreased to almost nothing where prisoners were worshiping Christ. I have worked side by side with those who once pedaled drugs and guns and even killed other people. More importantly, I have experienced God's forgiveness for my own despicable sins. Philip Yancey reminds us that if we were *"paid on the basis of fairness, we would all end up in hell."* If I can believe that God wants to forgive me, who am I to say that God is not gracious enough to forgive others?

Rob Bell, when asked if hell exists, considers the question from Lewis' "doors locked from the inside" view. *"Well, there are people now who are seriously separated from God. So I would assume that God will leave room for people to say "no I don't want any part of this." My question would be, does grace win or is the human heart stronger than God's love or grace. Who wins, does darkness and sin and hardness of heart win or does God's love and grace win?"*

The dogmatic universalists in the Christian world are relatively few. However, in speaking to other Christians about hell, I found that many of them are filled with hope; hope that Christ will save all the people we know and love and even those we don't; that God will show the same else. We hope that hell will not exist for ever, that God will remain slow to anger and quick to forgive, that no human being is infinitely sinful, and that the love of God will eventually conquer the universe. To close, we would do well to reflect on the musings of Friedrich Buechner:

"Dante saw written over the gates of hell the words `Abandon all hope ye who enter here', but he must have seen wrong. If there is suffering life in hell, there must also be hope in hell, because where there is life there is the Lord and giver of life, and where there is suffering he is there too because the suffering of the ones he loves is also his suffering.

`He descended into hell', the Creed says, and `If I make my bed in Sheol, thou art there', the Psalmist, David writes. (Psalm 139:8) It seems there is no depth to which he will not sink. Maybe not even Old Scratch will be able to hold out against him forever."

Conclusion:

This conclusion has been the most difficult portion of these pages to write. In a sense, I have found no conclusion. Just as when I started this book, I have not found a position on hell I can wholeheartedly endorse, and I am still troubled on occasion by the doctrine. I have found many reasons to question the traditional views of hell, but when I hear a preacher speak on eternal fire and the dreadful wrath of God, I still fear that I am wrong to question, and that my heresies will one day be discussed in front of the Judgment Seat of Christ. I can only hope that God will pardon my ignorance as well as my questions. I am forced to agree in frustration with Philip Yancey, who writes that "*I must insist that the most important questions about heaven and hell — who goes where, whether there are second chances, what form the judgments and rewards take, intermediate states after death — are opaque at best*". On the other hand, writing these pages has allowed me to grapple with the belief, to explore alternate legitimate versions of belief in hell, and perhaps to understand a little more. I know that I am not alone in this struggle. Since I began writing about this topic, hell has become one of the hot topics (no pun intended) of the Christian community in North America, with the debate on its nature raging even in secular and popular media.

I believe it is important to contend with the doctrine of hell, even for those of us who will never be completely comfortable with it. I believe the church does itself no favors by ignoring hell, as it so often does. Hell is an integral part of our theology, of how we think and behave as Christians. Hell is a driving force behind our drive to "share Jesus" with others, a helpful reminder to keep us from sin, a deterrent to accepting different or heretical ideas, and a subtle influence on the way we treat others. If we believe in heaven and hell, it must affect us.

C.S. Lewis wrote that *"it is a serious thing to live in a society of possible gods and goddesses, to remember that the dullest and most uninteresting person you can talk to may one day be a creature which, if you saw it now, you would be strongly tempted to worship, or else a horror and a corruption such as you now meet, if at all, only in a nightmare. All day long we are, in some degree, helping each other to one or other of these destinations"*. Consciously or sub-consciously, our belief in hell will manifest itself.

I hope that by reading this book, you may join me inspecting and re-evaluating our belief in hell. Hell is too important, too valuable an idea to smolder in our subconscious, to affect us quietly. Do we really believe that most will be eternally tortured? If we do, that should become the guiding principle in our lives. Nothing should matter to us but snatching them out of the fire, and we should tremble with fear lest we too are headed to hell. If we cannot accept such a belief, we should not quietly ignore it, but rather try to understand where we are wrong and correct the belief as best we can, so that we can once again say confidently that we believe *"he will come again to judge the living and the dead."*

I think these pages have only scratched the surface in understanding the doctrine of hell throughout church history. Every concept explored here has been the subject of thick books and intense study from serious theologians. There are important and controversial doctrines- predestination and the inerrancy of Scripture particularly- that I have deliberately skirted around. I hope that both those who believe in divine election and those who do not, those who believe that the Scriptures are inerrant and those that don't, will find something of value here.

The very short stories at the beginnings of each chapter were stories that affected me, each in their own way, in thinking through hell. Some of them are well-known, while others have never been published, and not all of them are directly about hell; but they are each in their own way important to me. Hopefully, they help others to think as well.

In terms of my own conclusions, it should be clear from my writings that I lean towards inclusive salvation, a metaphorical view of hell itself and the possibility of salvation after death. Nonetheless, I realize those ideas raise both Biblical and practical concerns. I hope that all readers will come to their own conclusions on this vital issue of hell, rather than simply accepting mine. I have not tried, particularly, to hide my own biases, but I have attempted to provide solid scriptural references and formidable defenders for all the major views on hell so that people can use them as a springboard for their own study.

Though I used many sources and spoke with many people in preparing to write, the following were particularly useful to me. The sermons of Jonathan Edwards provided a vivid, eloquent and intelligent defense of the fiercest possible view of hell. The William Crockett - edited "Four Views on Hell" showcased four Bible scholars debating the literal, metaphorical, purgatorial and conditional views. The works of C.S. Lewis provide a wealth of ideas that have drastically impacted how modern Christians understand hell; it is nowadays common to hear someone say they have a "Lewis view" on hell or a "Last Battle" view of salvation. Brian McLaren's "The Last Word and the Word After That" features fictional characters working through many of the same moral, emotional, theological and Biblical issues I have raised in my writing. The website tentmaker.org provides a wealth of information, along with invaluable quotations, for those interested in universalism. William Barclay provides interesting verse-by-verse analysis of the New Testament, including those verses dealing with hell and salvation. My good friend "Jacob", whose blog www.twentyfeet.blogspot.com is a treasure trove for those struggling with traditional Christian faith, gave me both questions and answers through the many discussions we had about hell. Finally there is my wife Kathryn, who is not quoted in this book, but whose solid faith and steadfast belief that understanding God's love is more important than the details of hell keep me sane when I am struggling.

Brian McLaren suggested that our view of hell is less important than the view of God it leads to, and I have found him to be correct. Many Christian teachings are difficult or unclear to me, but only hell had the power to make me doubt the love and goodness of God. I could not, and cannot reject the doctrine outright - both for Biblical reasons and because I do believe in final accountability, but hell made it difficult for me to love God, to trust God, to follow God in the ways that He asks me to.

Through much research and discussion I have found ways to understand hell that I consider reasonable (or at least defensible), that highlight both the awful sin of mankind and the glorious grace of God, that show that mercy and justice are not opposed but rather complimentary facets of a God that loves us all. If my findings be heretical or untrue, they are at least untruths that have helped point me to the greatest truth of all, the truth that God really is good. I may not have found one clear answer to the problem of hell, but I have found that I can believe, more often than not, that God has, and that God's answers will make sense to me when I finally do get them. And I can believe, truly believe, that God is Love and that He loves humanity and wants the best for us, then everything else will fall into place.

Acknowledgements

First of all, thank you to the many who have struggled with, meditated on and written about this subject before. I am deeply grateful for their guidance.
Thank you to Estelle, for all the editing and formatting I was unwilling to do.
Thank you to Joel, Benny, and Stan, and everybody in my family, for allowing me to talk through such a cheerless subject with them again and again.
Finally, thank you always to Kathryn and my little ones, for keeping me sane and happy. You truly are God's gift to me.

About the Author

Jens lives in Manitoba, Canada with his wife and two children

Bibliography:

1. Abraham, Mark (Editor). Improbable Research, http://improbable.com/ig/ig-pastwinners.html, last visited November 17, 2010.
2. Aiken, Mercy and Gary Arimault. "Honest Questions and Answers about Hell" at Tentmaker, http://www.tentmaker.org/articles/ifhellisreal.htm. Last Visited December 1, 2010.
3. "Aimiel" posting on "to all Christians: If there were no hell, would you still be a Christian?" thread of *theologyonline.com*, http://www.theologyonline.com/forums/showthread.php?t=47197&page=7. Posted March 17, 2008. Last visited December 1, 2010.
4. Aligheri, Dante. *The Divine Comedy*, 1555. English edition found at http://www.everypoet.com/archive/poetry/dante/ Translated by Henry Wadsworth Longfellow, 1987.
5. Amalric, Amoud. Quote found on Wikipedia page http://en.wikipedia.org/wiki/Arnaud_Amalric#cite_note-1, Last Modified 29 October 2010, Last visited November 29, 2010.
6. "Anne V". *A Letter from a Soul From Hell*, These Last Days Ministries at http://www.tldm.org/news6/hell2.htm. Last Updated February 3, 2010. Last visited November 29, 2010
7. Atkinson, Gordon. "A Preacher, a Rabbi and a Professor go into a Computer Store", *Real Live Preacher*, at http://www.barnesandnoble.com/w/reallivepreachercom-gordon-atkinson/1006448431?ean=9780802828101 (Last visited Dec 12, 2014,)
8. Atkinson, Gordon. "Hell, Video 1", https://www.youtube.com/watch?v=k7x6xbYey04
Hell Video 3 https://www.youtube.com/watch?v=N_Z5a20NLck
Hell video 4 https://www.youtube.com/watch?v=dD27wcIaRwc

(Last visited Dec 12, 2014, 2014).
9. Atwater, MH." Is There a Hell? Surprising Observations About the Near-Death Experience" in *The Journal of Near-Death Studies* Volume 10 No. 3, 1992.
10. Augustine of Hippo. Quoted by Philip Gulley and James Mulholland in *If Grace is True: Why God will Save Every Person*, Harper-Collins Publishers, 2003.
11. Augustine of Hippo. The City of God. Translated by Marcus Dods, Digireads.com Publishing, 2009. Found online at http://books.google.ca/books?id=Xl5qY9BFhrQC&pg=PA567&lpg=PA567&dq=augustine+arguing+for+eternal+punishment&source=bl&ots=dgX_EvB_wJ&sig=-optDX-oqfF5lA0PYnIdoh9bgNE&hl=en&ei=1332TMsJgpecB7DdtfYK&sa=X&oi=book_result&ct=result&resnum=2&ved=0CB0Q6AEwAQ#v=onepage&q&f=false.
12. Aquinus, Thomas. *Summa Theologica, Third Part, Supplement, Question XCIV*, "Of the Relations of the Saints Towards the Damned," First Article, "Whether the Blessed in Heaven Will See the Sufferings of the Damned. . ." 1265-1274.
13. Barclay, William. A Spiritual Autobiography, William B. Erdmann's Publishing Company, Grand Rapids, 1977. The relevant section can be found online at http://www.auburn.edu/~allenkc/barclay1.html. Last Visited November 29, 2010.
14. Barclay, William. *Commentary on The Revelation of John*. Westminster Press, 1976.
Barclay, William. Quoted at "Universalism Through Church History" at *Tentmaker*, *http://www.tentmaker.org/Quotes/uniquotes.htm*. Last visited December 1, 2010.
15. Barclay, William. *The Gospel of Matthew, Volumes One and Two*, (the Daily Bible Study Series, Revised Edition). 1957, revised by St. Andrew's Press, 2001.
16. Barclay, William. *The Letter to the Romans (New Daily Study Bible)* third edition, St. Andrew's Press, 2002.
17. Barclay, William. *The Letters of James and Peter: The New Daily Study Bible*, third edition, St. Andrew's Press, 2003.
18. Baxter, Mary K. *A Divine Revelation of Hell*. Lowery Ministries International, 1993. Full text can be found online at

http://spiritlessons.com/mary_k_baxter_a_divine_revelation_of_hell.htm

19. Beecher, Edward. *History of Opinions on the Scriptural Doctrine of Retribution.* D. Appleton and Company, 1878.

20. Bell, Rob. "Bullhorn" Nooma Video, http://www.youtube.com/watch?v=-ouz24ibMiI&feature=related, 11 April, 2007. Last visited November 29, 2010.

21. Bell, Rob. Interview with Vic Cuccia, July 3, 2007. Interview found at http://planetpreterist.com/content/interview-rob-bell . Last Visited December 1, 2010.

22. Bell, Rob. *Love Wins,* HarperOne, 2011.

23. "Bloody Mary" quote in Thomas Allen and Mark T. Chamberlain's *Every Knee Shall Bow,* xulonpress, 2005.

24. Buechner, Fredrich. *Wishful Thinking,* London: Collins, 1973

25. Bunyan, John. *Grace Abounding to the Chief of Sinners.* J.F. Dove, St. John's Square, 1857.

26. Chan, Francis. *Erasing Hell: What God Said about Eternity, and the Things We Made Up.* David C. Cook, 2011.

27. Coulter, Ann. *Godless: the Church of Liberalism.* Crown Forum, 2006.

28. Craig, William Lane. Can a Loving God Send People to Hell? A debate between Craig and Ray Bradley. 1994. Found at http://www.ovrlnd.com/Universalism/Craig_Bradley_Debate.html.

29. Crockett, William with John Walvoord, Zachary Hayes, Clark Pinnock. *Four Views on Hell.* Zondervan, 1996.

30. Dawkins, Richard. "Religion's Real Child Abuse" at The Richard Dawkins Foundation, https://richarddawkins.net/2013/01/physical-versus-mental-child-abuse/

31. Diodore of Tarsus. Quoted by Mark T. Chamberlain and Thomas Allin in *Every Knee Shall Bow,* xulonpress, 2005.

32. Dobson, James. Interview with Ted Bundy on January 24, 1989. Interview found at Pure Intimacy, http://www.pureintimacy.org/piArticles/A000000433.cfm

33. Edwards, Jonathan. Edwards Works, Volume 8, p 166. Found at tentmaker quotes, 2010,

http://www.tentmaker.org/Quotes/hell-fire.htm
34. Edwards, Jonathan. Sermon entitled *Natural Men in a Dreadful Condition*. February, 1753. Found at http://www.gracegems.org/SERMONS/Edwards_dreadful.htm Last visited Dec 12, 2014.
35. Edwards, Jonathan. Sermon entitled *Sinners in the Hands of an Angry God*, July 8, 171. Found at Christian Classics Etheral Library at
http://www.ccel.org/ccel/edwards/sermons.sinners.html
36. Edwards, Jonathan. Sermon entitled *The Justice of God in the Damnation of Sinners*, 1734. Found at Christian Classics Etheral Library at
http://www.ccel.org/ccel/edwards/sermons.justice.html. Last visited Nov 19, 2010.
37. Fallwell, Jerry. Quoted by *Positive Atheism's Big Scary List of Jerry Fallwell Quotations*, http://www.positiveatheism.org/hist/quotes/foulwell.htm, Last Visited November 29, 2010.
38. Ferrem, Nels. Quoted by Willam Crockett in *Four Views on Hell*, Zondervan, 1996.
39. Finney, Rev. Charles G. "Why Sinners Hate God" in *Sermons on Important Subjects*. John S.Taylor Theological and Sunday School Bookseller, 1836. Sermon found online at http://articles.ochristian.com/article3744.shtml, Last Visited December 1, 2010.
40. Furmiss, J. *The Sight of Hell*, Kelly & Peit, 1864.
41. Geisler, Norman. Interview in Lee Strobel's *The Case For Faith: A Journalist Investigates the Toughest Objections to Christianity*. Zondervan, 2001.
42. Ghandi, Mohandas. Quotation found on Brainy Quote at http://www.brainyquote.com/quotes/quotes/m/mohandasga401593.html. Last visited November 17, 2010.
43. Global Media Outreach. The Four Spiritual Laws at http://www.godlovestheworld.com/. Last Visited November 17, 2010.
44. Graham, Billy. Interview with Robert Schuller. May 31, 1997. Audio at
http://www.christianfallacies.com/video/GrahamSchuller/GrahamSchuller.html, Last Visited Nov 19. 2010.

45. Graham, Billy. Quoted in Time Magazine, November 15, 1993.
46. Gulley, Philip and James Mulholland. *If Grace is True: Why God will Save Every Person*, Harper-Collins Publishers, 2003.
47. Habermas, Gary and JP Moreland. *Immortality: the Other Side of Death*. Thomas Nelson Inc, 1992
48. Hanson, Rev. John Wesley. T*he Greek Word Aion- Aionios Found Translated Everlasting-Eternal in the Holy Bible, Shown to Denote Limited Duration*. Northwestern Universalist Publishing House, 1875. Found online at http://www.tentmaker.org/books/Aion_lim.html.
49. Hontheim, Joseph. "Hell." The Catholic Encyclopedia. Vol. 7. New York: Robert Appleton Company, 1910. http://www.newadvent.org/cathen/07207a.htm
50. Ingersoll, Robert G." Lecture on the gods", 1876. Published in *Lectures of Col. R. G. Ingersoll, Vol 1*. The Echo Library, 2007
51. Ingersoll, Robert. *The Works of Robert G Ingersoll, Volume II*. New York, 1900.
52. Julian of Norwich. *Revelations of Divine Love*. Full Text Available at "Christian Classics Ethereal Library, http://www.ccel.org/ccel/julian/revelations. Last Visited November 29, 2010.
53. Kaplan, Andrew. *Scorpion*. MacMillan Publishing Company, 1986.
54. Kohler, Kauffman and Ludwig Blau. "Gehenna" in *Jewish Encyclopedia, http://www.jewishencyclopedia.com/view.jsp?artid=115&letter=G* , Last Visited November 29, 2010.
55. Lawhead, Stephen R. *Arthur*. Zondervan, 1996.
56. Lewis, Clive Staples. *Letters to Malcolm: Chiefly on Prayer*. Harvest Books, 1964.
57. Lewis, Clive Staples. *Mere Christianity*. Macmillan Publishers, 1952.
58. Lewis, Clive Staples. Personal Letter to Arthur Greeves, 1946. Quoted in James Townsend's "C.S. Lewis Theology: Somewhere Between Ransom and Reepicheep?" found at http://www.faithalone.org/journal/2000i/townsend2000e.htm, last visited November 29. 2010.

59. Lewis, Clive Staples. *Screwtape Letters*. Geoffrey Bles, 1942.
60. Lewis, Clive Staples. *The Great Divorce*. Geoffrey Bles, 1945.
61. Lewis, Clive Stapes. *The Weight of Glory*. HarperOne, 1949.
62. Lewis, Clive Staples. *The Problem of Pain*, 1947. reprinted by Kessinger Publication, 2004.
63. Lewis, Clive Staples. *The Last Battle.* The Bodley Head, 1956.
64. Lucado, Max. *In the Grip of Grace*. Thomas Nelson, 1996.
65. Lucado, Max. *3:16: The Numbers of Hope*. Thomas Nelson, 2007.
66. Luther, Martin. Quoted by William Curtis Holzen in *A Critical and Constructive Defense of the Salvic Optimism of Inclusivism*, January 2005. http://uir.unisa.ac.za/bitstream/handle/10500/1891/dissertation.pdf?sequence=1
67. Lutzer, Erwin W. *One Minute After You Die: A Preview of Your Final Destination*. Moody Publishers, 1997.
68. Macdonald, William. Quoted by Joel Short on "The Problem with Hell", *Twenty Feet*, http://twentyfeet.blogspot.com/2006/11/problem-with-hell.html (Jan 31, 2007)(Last visited November 17, 2010)
69. Martyr, Justin. Quoted in Clark Pinnock's A Wideness *in God's Mercy: the finality of Jesus Christ in a World of Religion*. Zonderzan, 1992.
70. McCabe, Joseph. *History of Torture*. Amer Atheist Press, 1982.
71. McKaig, Charles on Dr. Maurice Rawling's film *to Hell and Back*. Video found at http://www.divinerevelations.info/documents/rawlings/dr_rawlings_near_death_experiences.htm Last Visited November 29, 2010.
72. McLaren, Brian. *The Last Word and the Word After That*. Jossey-Bass, 2005.   73. Messandé, G. "*The History of the Devil*", Newell, London, England. 1996.
74. Micheal, Sherif. "Angels of Light" , *Earth Harvest,* found at *http://www.earthharvest.org/en/christian_online_bible_apologetics/whoisgod/8BibleWitchesWitchcraftNewAgeFalseProphetsYoga.htm.* Last visited November 17, 2010.

75. Milton, John. *Paradise Lost*. Samuel Simmons, 1667.
76. Moreland, JP. Interview in Lee Storbel's *The Case For Faith: A Journalist Investigates the Toughest Objections to Christianity*. Zondervan, 2001.
77. Morris, Henry M. and, Martin E. Clark. *The Bible Has the Answer, Revised Edition*. Master Books, 1976.
78. Origen, *de Principees,* Book 1, Chapter 6. Quoted by Mercy Aiken at Tentmaker, http://www.tentmaker.org/biographies/origen.htm, last visited December 1, 2010.
79. Paine, Thomas. *The Theological Works*. JP Mendum, Investigator Office Boston. 1859.
80. Perreti, Frank. Radio Interview with Dr. James Dobson on "Focus on the Family". Transcribed from memory.
81. Phelps, Fred. *God Hates Fags* at https://www.youtube.com/watch?v=ThUC1Q7rX4k
82. Pope John Paul II. "Hell is the State of All Those who Reject God" translated from Losservatore Romano on CatholicCulture.org, http://www.catholicculture.org/culture/library/view.cfm?id=1183 (speech on July 28, 1999).
83. Rahner, Karl. Quote found at "Anonymous Christian" on Wikipedia, http://en.wikipedia.org/w/index.php?title=Anonymous_Christian&oldid=171253832#cite_note-Clinton-0, 13 Nov 2007.
84. Rawlings, Maurice. *Beyond Death's Door*. Bantam Books, 1979.
85. Rawlings, Maurice. *To Hell and Back*. Found at http://spiritlessons.com/Documents/Rawlings/Dr_Rawlings_Near_Death_Experiences.htm. last Visited November 29, 201
86. Reese, Thomas. Quoted in Jeffrery L. Sheller's "Hell Has no Fury", *US News and World Report*, January 31, 2000
87. Reuter, Estelle. *Following God's Call- living among the Zulus*, Blurb 2014
88. Richmond, Gary. *All God's Creatures*. W Pub Group, 1991.
89. Russel, Bertrand. *Why I am not a Christian*, 1967. Full text found at http://users.drew.edu/~jlenz/whynot.html, last visited November 29, 2010.
90. Short, Joel. "About Hell and Stuff Like That", Twenty Feet,

http://twentyfeet.blogspot.com/2004/12/about-hell-and-stuff-like-that.html December 10, 2004. (Last visited November 17, 2010.)
91. Short, Joel. "Amazing Grace", *Twenty Feet*, http://twentyfeet.blogspot.com/2006/03/amazing-grace.html (March 7, 2006)(Last visited November 29, 2010)
96. Short, Joel. "Hell and Justice" at *Twenty Feet*, http://twentyfeet.blogspot.com/2007/09/hell-and-justice.html (September 26, 2007) (Last visited November 18, 2010)
92. Short, Joel. "I chose Love", *Twenty Feet*, http://twentyfeet.blogspot.com/2007/08/i-choose-love.html, (Aug 6, 2007)(Last visited November 29, 2010)
93. Short, Joel. "The Problem with Hell", *Twenty Feet*, http://twentyfeet.blogspot.com/2006/11/problem-with-hell.html (Jan 31, 2007)(Last visited November 17, 2010).
94. Slagle, Charles. "Does Jesus Really Love Little Children?" at *tentmaker*, http://www.tentmaker.org/FAQ/DoesJesusREALLYLoveLittleChildren.html
last visited Dec 12, 2014
95. Sproul, RC. *Essential Truths of the Christian Faith*. Tyndale House, 1992.
96. Sproul, RC. "God in the Hands of Angry Sinners", By His Grace, http://www.gracesermons.com/robbeeee/angry.html, updated Feb 4, 2009.
97. Spurgeon, C.H. Sermon entitled "The Resurrection of the Dead", February 17, 1856. Found at The Spurgeon Archive by Philip R. Johnson, 2001 at http://www.spurgeon.org/sermons/0066.htm
98. Spurgeon, CH. Sermon entitled "The Wailing of Risca" preached December 9, 1860. Found at The Spurgeon Archives by Philip E. Johnson, 2001.
http://www.spurgeon.org/sermons/0349.htm
99. Sullivan, K (director). *Anne of Green Gables*, CBC, 1985.
100. Storm, Howard. "Saved from Hell: Rev. Howard Storm's Near-Death Experiene" at *Near-Death Experiences and the Afterlife*, 2007. Found at http://www.near-death.com/storm.html, Last Visited November 29, 2010
101. Swedenborg, Emmanuel. *Heaven and Hell, 1758.* Translated from Latin by George F. Dole, Swedenborg

Foundation, 1991.
102. Talbot, Thomas in Robin A. Perry and Christopher Hugh Partridge's *Universal Salvation? The Current Debate*. W.B. Erbman's Publishing Company, 2003
103. Teilhard de Chardin as quoted by Rev. Leo Watt, *Hell: A Modern Approach,* Melbourne: ACTS Publications, 1967.
104. Tertullian. *De Spectaculis, Chapter XXX.* (197-202).
105. Unknown author. "Scientific Explanation of Hell", received by email on January 4, 2006. I have some sexual content out of the last few lines to avoid causing unnecessary offense
106. Van Impe, Jack. *Revelation Revealed*. Jack Van Impe Ministries, 1982.
107. Van Nattan, Mary. "CS Lewis: The Devil's Wisest Fool", The Home Maker's Corner, at http://www.homemakerscorner.com/cslewis.htm. Last visited November 17, 2010.
108. Vincent, Ken. Quoted by Mercy Aiken, "Do Near-Death Experiences Confirm the Existence of Hell" at tentmaker, http://www.tentmaker.org/FAQ/NDE-hell.htm. Last Visited November 29, 2010.
109. Washer, Paul. "All Men are Born Evil". Retrieved on November 18, 2010 from http://www.youtube.com/watch?v=mEOqxibhCxU&playnext=1&list=PL67E720644CF2FCA8&index=41
110. Washer, Paul. "The Holiness of God part II". Retrieved on November 19, 2010 from http://www.youtube.com/watch?v=6VeawfXAgzQ
111. Watts, Isaac. Quoted by Gary Arimault, *Quotes from Christian Perpetuators of the Mythology of Hell* at http://www.tentmaker.org/Quotes/hell-fire.htm. Last visited on November 29, 2010.
112. Wesley, John. "On Living Without God", *The Works of John Wesley*, 1872.
113. Yancey, Philip. *Reaching for the Invisible God*. Zondervan, 2000.
114. Yancey, Philip. *Rumors of Another World: What on Earth are We Missing?* Zondervan, 2003.
115. Yancey, Philip. *Soul Survivor: How my Faith Survived the Church"*. Hodder & Stoughton, 2001.

116. Yancey, Philip. *What's so Amazing About Grace?* Zondervan, 1987
117. Yancey, Philip. *Where is God when it Hurts?* Zondervan, 1977.
118. Yohannan, KP and William Booth and CT Studd are quoted at *The Bible Channel* on http://www.thebiblechannel.org/Missions_Quotes/missions_quotes.html
119. Zacharias, Ravi. Interview in Lee Strobel's *The Case For Faith: A Journalist Investigates the Toughest Objections to Christianity.* Zondervan, 2001.

Endnotes with Bible references

Chapter 1
[1] Romans 3:10
[2] Deuteronomy 32:35
[3] John 3:19
[4] Luke 10:13
[5] Matthew 23 : 33-34
[6] Revelation 20:7-10

Chapter 2
[7] Matthew 25:31-46
[8] Ecclesiastes 9:2-6
[9] Daniel 12:2
[10] Matthew 16:18
[11] Barclay, William
[12] Mark 9:48
[13] Matthew 13:42
[14] Matthew 18:8
[15] Matthew 18:35
[16] Matthew 22:13

[17] Matthew 23:32
[18] Matthew 25:41
[19] Matthew 25:46

Chapter 3
[20] Matt: 8:12, 22:13, 25:30
[21] Jude 1:13
[22] 2 Thessalonians 1:7
[23] Jeremiah 7:31
[24] 1 Corinthians 13:12

Chapter 4
[25] Revelations 12:7-9
[26] Genesis 3:1-6
[27] Job 2:6
[28] Luke 10:18
[29] Matthew 16:18
[30] 2 Corinthians 11: 13-14

Chapter 5
[31] John 14:6
[32] Luke 23:40-42
[33] John 11:26
[34] Matthew 7:13-14
[35] Mark 16:16
[36] Acts 4:12
[37] John 3:18
[38] Matthew 19:14
[39] Romans 10:13
[40] Matthew 13: 24-30
[41] Samson 16:28
[42] Romans 2:5-10
[43] Acts 10:34
[44] Luke 13:23-30
[45] Matthew 19:26

Chapter 6
[46] 2 Corinthians 5:10

[47] 1Corinthians 1:10-15
[48] Luke 12:47
[49] Revelations 14:9-10
[50] Revelation 20:10
[51] Matthew 18:34
[52] Mark 9 :44
[53] 2 Thessalonians 1:9
[54] Jude 1:7
[55] 1 Peter 4:8
[56] Luke 6:27-31
[57] Matthew 5:43-48

Chapter 7
[58] Mark 8:36
[59] Matthew 18:9
[60] Luke 12:5
[61] Matthew 25:36

Chapter 8
[62] Revelation 21:8
[63] Luke16:19-31
[64] Isaiah 66:23
[65] Matthew 10:28

Chapter 10
[66] Psalm 139:8
[67] Ezekiel 16:53
[68] Roman 11:8
[69] Roman 11:25-32
[70] Matthew 25:46
[71] 1Peter3:18-20
[72] 1Peter 4:5-6
[73] Romans 5:18
[74] 1 Timothy 2:4
[75] 2 Peter 3:9
[76] Psalm 103:8-9
[77] Ezekiel 18:23
[80] Isaiah 8:21-22

[81] Isaiah 9:1-2

Printed in Great Britain
by Amazon.co.uk, Ltd.,
Marston Gate.